'To read this expansive treasure
differently. Personal, pressing
writing and thinking on every p
— **Sabrina Mahfouz, author of** *These Bodies of Water*

'This act of devotion could not be possible without honesty and vulnerability, which illuminates a form of embodied knowing rooted in The Divine. It is a gift and a blessing for anyone who has ever faced invisibility and over-scrutiny at the same time; a healing dedication to those who have been marked as different or forced to contort themselves into spaces where they don't fit. In these loving pages, we are encouraged to want more and see ourselves for ourselves.'
— **Muneera Pilgrim, author of** *That Day She'll Proclaim Her Chronicles*

'A rare, contemporary work of literature-as-prayer that moves the heart and provokes thought in equal measure. Manzoor-Khan offers us a profoundly personal meditation and an important reaffirmation that faith can be a solace and a guide through the performative demands of modern life.'
— **Preti Taneja, author of** *Aftermath*

'*Seeing for Ourselves* is a rare treat. As Suhaiymah Manzoor-Khan adds layer upon layer to her reflections, we witness a profound thinker and remarkable poet at work.'
— **Arun Kundnani, author of** *What Is Antiracism?*

'Utterly disruptive. With grace and vulnerability, and through the use of gorgeous prose, Manzoor-Khan upends the conversation on representational politics, encouraging us instead to think along lines that are both spiritually and materially liberating.'
— **Waithera Sebatindira, author of** *Through an Addict's Looking-Glass*

SEEING FOR
OURSELVES

First published in 2023
by Hajar Press C.I.C., London, United Kingdom
www.hajarpress.com
@hajarpress

ISBN 978-1-914221-22-4 Paperback
ISBN 978-1-914221-23-1 EPUB eBook

A Cataloguing-in-Publication data record for this
book is available from the British Library.

Cover and interior art: Han Gunji Stephens
Cover design: Samara Jundi
Typesetting: Laura Jones / lauraflojo.com

Printed and bound in the United Kingdom by
Clays Ltd, Elcograf S.p.A.

SEEING FOR OURSELVES

AND EVEN STRANGER POSSIBILITIES

SUHAIYMAH MANZOOR-KHAN

بِسْمِ ٱللَّهِ ٱلرَّحْمَٰنِ ٱلرَّحِيمِ

In the name of Allah, the Most Compassionate, the Most Merciful

ٱلْحَمْدُ لِلَّهِ رَبِّ ٱلْعَٰلَمِينَ

All praise is due to Allah, the Lord of all the worlds

اَللّٰهُمَّ صَلِّ عَلَىٰ سَيِّدِنَا مُحَمَّدٍ وَعَلَىٰ آلِهِ وَصَحْبِهِ وَسَلِّمْ

O Allah, send blessings and peace upon our master
Muhammad and upon his family and companions

for everyone who has lost something (and who among us hasn't?)
for the public libraries and all who sit lonely within them
for the chai shops open late and all who laugh loudly inside them
for everyone wishing for more than this lesser life
for my people, whatever makes you that
for the intentions, because they are all that count
for hope of mercy and acceptance

إِنَّمَا الْأَعْمَالُ بِالنِّيَّاتِ وَإِنَّمَا لِكُلِّ امْرِئٍ مَا نَوَى

Actions are according to their intentions,
and everyone will get what was intended.[1]

Contents

١

THE NEED /
HOW I AM FOUND

ACT I: SCENE I

the writer and the book stand opposite each other, mirroring one another. If either one has a body distinct from the other, we cannot tell. They are in a beautiful public library that is dissolving around them. Time is a metaphor of dappled light coming through a window in the ceiling.

the writer   You're not what I thought you were going to be

the book   What did you expect?

the writer   You were supposed to be about seeing and being seen
About the different gazes upon us
and how to see ourselves without them

the book looks smirkingly at the writer, knowing more than her (as always).

the book   Is that not what I am?

the writer   Well, it's just
you seem more preoccupied with what *I* am
than with being what I want you to be

Pause.

the book   Is that so different from what you expected?

They stare at each other for a long time. Eventually, the writer cannot keep it up.

the writer   Stop looking at me!

At the beginning of *Black Skin, White Masks*, Frantz Fanon asks, 'Why am I writing this book? Nobody asked me to. Especially not those for whom it is intended.'[1] Many writers inspired by his work have opened their own books with a similar question. But I cannot. I was asked to write this book by Hajar Press, and that is probably the most honest place to start.

At the same time, nobody asked me to write these specific contents, and so the question of motivation has haunted my writing. If I had written this book not knowing it would be published, I would be confident that its purpose was solely to help me to think. I would be able to state that the reason I wrote this was to work through how I might extract myself from the gazes I am ensnared in.

Indeed, at some level, this is what most of my writing to date has been working through. And the working-through never quite 'ends' because my navigation of gazes is itself exposed to gazes as I share my work publicly. I perform poetry, deliver my thoughts to rooms of people and write words that are printed. This means that not only is my thinking gazed upon, but *I am*, too. And in turn, the gazes that accumulate upon me when I share my thinking are iterations of gazes that are upon me even when I don't: eyes that demand, constrain and scrutinise.

This all multiplies the number of gazes that I find myself navigating, which makes it difficult to truly exit the pursuit. Therefore, I cannot claim that I write solely to think. My writing also attempts to pre-empt thoughts and responses to my thinking, as well as to the fact that it is me who is thinking.

And so the fact I have written this book knowing that it will be published means the writing has become entangled in the very process I hoped to dissect. I began wanting to write about how we might learn to see ourselves as more than objects that are looked at. How we might get beyond an analysis of where the gazes that constrain us come from and why we internalise them, instead reaching somewhere where we can develop our own modes of seeing: how to be subjects instead of objects.

But I soon found myself bored by this pursuit. It felt done and overdone—from W.E.B. Du Bois to Frantz Fanon to Audre Lorde to more recent navigations of contemporary racialising gazes. How had I found myself in the same position that writers had been in for over a century? And what could I bring to the question of gazes that would be new? And why did I want to? Would it impact the way I could actually *live*?

Troubled by such doubts, I started to consider why being a subject rather than an object was the furthest horizon I could dream of. What lay beyond 'seeing with my own eyes'? What if 'seeing for ourselves' wasn't actually the best way to see? What could transcend the desire to be see-er instead of seen? What if I closed my eyes and did not prioritise seeing at all?

As I began to lean into these stranger possibilities, the book morphed before me. Unwieldy and strange, it brought me to questions I had not dared to utter aloud before. My soul became ardent that *it* had more relevance to the question of how to live than my eyes did. And my heart took over navigation that I had so far delegated to my head.

In this, I was made aware of a major discrepancy in my writing to date. In focusing on the gazes upon me, I had neglected to seriously consider the gaze that at other times I professed was the most prominent and crucial in my life: the gaze of God. I now became aware that Allah's sight might be the only place where I could overcome the binary of subject-hood and objecthood. It might be the possibility of the further horizon I was seeking.

But how to write that?

How to allow all parts of myself congruency in an industry that has taught us to read within clear-cut genres? How, when we expect writers to present answers and routes to reading, rather than reveal that they are mid-journey themselves? How, with all the norms and boundaries imposed on our minds, in a context that teaches us that 'faith' must be severed from 'intellectual' or 'artistic' writing?

In other words, how to be truly truthful?

It was James Baldwin who said he wanted to be an honest man and a good writer. But the two do not always go hand in hand. For how honest can you be with language? Even as I write these paragraphs on being truthful, I wonder which parts of myself I am masking. Am I attempting to sound more certain than I feel? How bare is bearable?

I recall the first time I received feedback on a play I had spent months writing. I was nervous, but I believed in the story and the characters. So it came as a shock when the director suggested that, whilst my male character was flawed and therefore believable, my female character was not fleshed out enough.

My cheeks flushed red. How could it be? How could I have fallen prey to the misogynistic trope that I denounce others for? How could I have so severely let down my Muslim woman character?

I began to distrust my writing. I questioned if this meant that I did not see the women in my life as having the same complexity that I saw in the men. But upon deeper consideration, I came to realise that the sketchiness of my female character was my way of trying to protect her.

In a world so over-scrutinising of Muslim women, my instinct was to mask her interior world. So, yes, details about her family were sparse, and she did not have emotional outbursts or overt flaws. But was this dishonest of me? Or was it an all too honest reflection of what it is to write in a world of misogyny and Islamophobia?

Some days later, as I walked around the lake in my local park thinking about the feedback, it hit me that even in a fictional world of my own making, I did not feel it was safe for a Muslim woman to be flawed. Did this mean, at some level, that I did not believe the world could understand a Muslim woman to be both imperfect and loveable?

. This question caught me off guard. It was too revealing. Too honest. Too much to consider. I felt I would do better just to write my character with more outbursts and mentions of family. And so, perhaps good writing can come at the expense of being truly truthful sometimes, because being honest about honesty is remarkably difficult.

In fact, faced with the question of how to write this book in a way that allowed all parts of myself into the investigation of gazes, I faltered. I found no clear answer and no easy route, other than eventually just to try. To trust that I cannot be alone in my desire to seek a further horizon. To trust that somebody somewhere has also found themselves bored of the spiral of gazes you can spend a lifetime trying to navigate. And to trust that a reader does not have to share my experience or destination to appreciate the value of my journey.

After all, I believe writing has a responsibility to be worthwhile. I cannot be like those who believe in art for art's sake. And yet ... *responsibility.* What a boring word! It makes you want to throw a brick through a window, in honesty. But there it is, something you must think about. Perhaps it is the wrong word, but I will let it hold the place of a better word until we come up with one.

The poet Nayyirah Waheed states, 'that thing you are most afraid to write, write that.'[2] And to a great extent, I have tried. But as a believer in responsibility, the question I land on is *why?* If there are things we are afraid to write, it is surely important to ask why we are afraid to write them. Some fears may be mere expressions of self-doubt or worries about how we will be perceived, but there are also other fears that could be important to listen to.

For instance, the reason I am afraid to write some of the things that I'm afraid to write is because they are not mine to write. The fear is one of betrayal. A fear of misconstruction, co-option or over-exposure. A fear of causing pain to someone I love—deliberately or not—because anything I write relating to me is not my story alone; none of our stories are. I am answerable to everybody whose story is nesting inside mine. And thus, what I write has consequences.

Islamic scholars have often considered the tongue to be the most dangerous limb of the body because of the disproportionate harm it causes. Some have even suggested that the multiple 'cages' our tongues are held behind (the teeth, the jaw, the lips) are symbols to take heed of. Few other body parts are so constrained, after all. As a result, tradition urges restraint in speech. And since the pen is also a type of tongue, every written utterance carries a weighty responsibility.

But beyond fear of being misunderstood or fear of being irresponsible with others' stories—both of which can ultimately be navigated through re-drafting—the fear that has haunted me most in writing this book is that of my own intention. By virtue of this book's publication, there is an audience to anticipate. And in Islam, an audience is often considered the first obstacle to sincere intentions.

A famous hadith (narration) on the authority of 'Umar ibn al-Khattab (may Allah be pleased with him) states that the Prophet Muhammad ﷺ said,

إِنَّمَا الْأَعْمَالُ بِالنِّيَّاتِ وَإِنَّمَا لِكُلِّ امْرِئٍ مَا نَوَى

Actions are according to their intentions, and everyone
will get what was intended.[3]

There has been much commentary about the meaning of this hadith. It was spoken by the Prophet ﷺ in the context of the migration of many of the first Muslims from Makkah to Medina in seventh-century Arabia. They were told that if they were migrating for the sake of Allah and His Messenger ﷺ, their deed would count as such, but if they were migrating for some worldly gain, then their action would count for its sake. Thus, the intention, rather than the act itself, determined the deed's value.

8

The importance of this hadith is such that Imam al-Shafi'i, one of the great imams, jurisprudents and poets of Islam, said it 'contains one third of all knowledge'. To take that seriously goes against all the conditioning by secular modernity that has persuaded me that the value of a book is in its reception, or outward gain. Instead, the hadith teaches that the primary value of this book lies in what I truly intend with it, which could never be known to anyone other than an All-Seeing being.

This is almost unimaginable in a context where 'winning the point' or 'dropping the mic' are determinants of the worth of most writing and speech. I was taught that 'valuable' meant that which will win the argument. That which will demonstrate that you are smart, savvy and witty, and that your opponent is ridiculous and uninformed. Cambridge Union, week two of university: stand up straight, *'this house believes _____'*. I don't remember what we debated, but the point was to win. Knowledge was to be selected for this purpose. Truth was collateral.

Contrast that with the prayer Imam al-Shafi'i used to make when entering a debate. It is reported that he said,

وَمَا نَاظَرْتُ أَحَدًا إلا وَلَمْ أُبَالِ بَيَّنَ اللَّهُ الْحَقَّ عَلَى لِسَانِي أَوْ لِسَانِهِ

I never debated with anyone but that I did not mind whether
Allah clarified the truth on my tongue or his tongue.[4]

This reveals another paradigm altogether: commitment to the establishment of truth above desire to be the one to establish it. Value determined by truth, not presentation.

I will not pretend that I am capable of writing to establish any sort of truth, even my own. But I do hope that what gives this book value is its heart and soul—its striving—because my preoccupation with how I write this book has become a preoccupation with how I live. This is not a book that demonstrates 'findings', then, but a book that attempts to allow me to live congruently by trying to address the question of gazes in the most honest, responsible and intentional way that I can, whilst balancing my fears, legitimate and illegitimate.

When I say I am attempting to write honestly, I don't just mean telling the truth. I mean sitting with the complexity of my truth, holding its hand and not flinching or attempting to shut it away. Recognising that I may even be misrecognising it. That what I think is truth is not truth, and that even as I try to capture and find it, I may not be best placed to articulate it. And then choosing which parts of what I find are mine to share and which parts are somebody else's to protect. Which parts I may never get to share, out of fear, maybe, but not a bad fear, maybe a fear that is necessary. That is so hard. Do you know how hard that is?

Sometimes when I think about responsibility, all I want is for the things I write to be destroyed completely and to never talk about them again.

Let me write with trust. Let me write as one who believes that I will die. Let me write with the confidence that none of my writing will save me, or stand between me and the fire. Let me write with passion that is as humiliated as it is electric. Let me write humble. Let me write knowing it is nothing. Let me write contradictions. Let me write loosely. Let me cut out the writing and stick it back in again. Let me write in circles and accept it as my fate. Let the circles run off the page and wrap around my mind until the page and I are so interwoven that I remember I too will return to dust. Let me write honestly. Let me write remembering that it will never mean as much to anybody else as it will to me. Let me write without legacy. Let me write hoping not to be held accountable. Let me write remembering I am accountable for every single letter. Let me write gratefully—for the ability to write, for the nerves that connect the mind-thought to the arm, to the hand, to the tapping on the keyboard, to the satisfying movement of words across this acrid screen. Let me write using words I am uncertain about. It matters less what the dictionary says they mean and more what I hope they could mean. Let me write not for anyone—what a hope, what a conceit! Let me write assured of how much this is for myself more than anyone else. Let me write remembering that I cannot breathe when I don't. Lord, let me write!

٢

THE WANT /
HOW I FIND MYSELF

The nineteen white IKEA boxes in my room cause me shame. When they are made visible by a friend curiously asking about their presence, I make a joke of their existence. I hide the seriousness of their aspiration behind a self-deprecating comment about being 'a bit of a hoarder'. More truthfully, every note in these boxes, every school exercise book, worn birthday card, torn letter, faded journal, scrawled-on envelope, unreadable receipt and ancient bus ticket is a type of evidence I cling to. Scraps of life and bureaucracy that bear witness to my living. Evidence I have existed.

I am afraid to let on about this in case it becomes obvious how afraid I am to go unseen. In case it becomes obvious how powerful it is to destroy a people's history. How catastrophic it is to leave them believing they are suspended. To eliminate their past, present and knowledge.

I don't keep the boxes in hopes of being understood—don't get me wrong. I am not calling to be made intelligible. Let the destinations of my buses go unknown! Burn the journals upon my death, please! Let my secrets stay with me, but not the fact I had them. Not the fact I wrote them down. Not the fact I went someplace, with someone, was recipient to gestures, moments, feelings, others. Not that I was here.

My mother fears her bedroom is full of clutter. In reality, it is full of proof. We joke that she carries a filing cabinet around in her rucksack. It is a joke that attempts to hide how imperative her role is. How without the care and attentiveness channelled through her, my grandparents would be far worse off. If something happened to my mother (may Allah avert all harm from her, ameen), I would not know what to do but to look through that rucksack and hope to find answers in the scribbles on envelope backs and doctors' letters.

*

There are more photographs on external hard drives and in yellowing albums than there are anywhere on display in our house. We profess that we will organise them all one day—print them, categorise them and chronologise them. But it doesn't matter if we do. Their existence, lining the floor of a bedroom, or stacked as bytes of data in black boxes, is what we clutch on to. Rarely do we look at them. But the thought of losing them is too much to consider.

WHAT DOES IT MEAN FOR A THOUGHT TO BE TOO MUCH TO CONSIDER?

'Operation Legacy' was the name of the British government's programme to systematically destroy and hide evidence of the atrocities of its empire once its colonies became independent. The purpose of the purge, stated in orders issued from Whitehall to colonial officials across Britain's occupied territories in 1961, was to prevent post-independence states from inheriting material that 'might embarrass' the British government, police, military forces, public servants or police informers.[1]

In practice, Operation Legacy entailed burning, burying and drowning thousands of colonial documents. Thousands more were shipped to Britain to be shelved in a secret archive whose existence was unlawfully hidden from the public for fifty years. In some cases, coded security classifications were even developed for the implementation of this elaborate process, ensuring clearance to handle certain files would only be entrusted to 'British officers of European descent'.[2]

The dictionary defines 'embarrass' as 'to cause someone to feel nervous, worried, or uncomfortable'. A family member behaving inappropriately in public. Somebody mentioning a private detail about you to a stranger. Being complimented unexpectedly. But the discovery by people that you colonised of documents that detail your occupation, brutalisation and expropriation of them is not embarrassment. That is the possibility of being held to account. That is the possibility of calls for rightful reparation.[3]

The destruction of the records of empire aimed to reduce colonial violence to the level of mere allegation. Unevidenced claims. Anecdotal versions of the past. Blurry recollections. Not history.

This was ensured not only by destroying the evidence, but by destroying evidence of the destruction of the evidence. British authorities sought to avoid the situation that had arisen in India in 1947, when local media had caught on to the mass incineration of colonial documents as a 'pall of smoke' fell over Delhi. Subsequently, in 1961 British civil servants were instructed to burn papers in such a way that 'the waste should be reduced to ash and the ashes broken up'. In some cases, instruction was given to pack files into 'weighted crates' to be 'dumped in very deep and current-free water at maximum practicable distance from the coast'.[4]

Operation Legacy is one of the starkest illustrations of the fact that *we don't know what we don't know about history* not only due to accident, lack of literary sources, death of oral narrators, or insufficient recording of the past, but also because of deliberate erasure, and erasure of that erasure.

As I was preparing my morning oats one evening, a documentary began to auto-play on my phone. An Indigenous woman from Greenland was on a quest to uncover what the Danish government had done to a generation of Greenlandic women in the 1960s–1970s. Her mission had been prompted by the memory of a single day.

She was thirteen. Girls were being taken out of the school classroom one by one. Eventually her turn came. She was led to a room where—with neither her consent nor the knowledge of a parent—doctors told her to remove her underpants and then forced an IUD contraceptive device into her child-sized uterus. She had no idea what was happening, or why, or what the impact would be. She would only remember the immensity of the pain— like being stabbed by knives. After the procedure she went back to her desk, and the next girl was taken out of class.

Years later, the documentary identified this woman's memory as part of the Danish government's forcible sterilisation campaign of Indigenous Greenlandic girls. The documentary explained that the campaign remains under prolonged investigation partially because of the difficulty of accessing relevant historical records. When I heard this, the phrase 'forcible forgetting' came to my mind. Not only had these women's bodies been violated with the intent of ethnic cleansing and Indigenous genocide, but their memories of the violence were all they had as evidence to usher in an investigation in the first place.

The part of the documentary that struck me most was when a group of women, now in their sixties, reflected on the pain of never knowing why they couldn't get pregnant. For years, doctors told them they were healthy and fertile, that nothing was 'wrong'. How unbearable must it have been for those women to discover not only that they were violated as children, but also that they were denied any information about the impact the IUD would have on their lives. Some had forgotten or suppressed the memory of the insertion, not realising they had something inside their bodies. Their uteruses remained the only conscious witnesses. The only archive.

It was in the writing of Postcolonial Studies scholars that I first came across the idea that *we don't know what we don't know about history*. At the time, I was recording oral histories of women like my grandmother who migrated from Pakistan to Leeds and Bradford in the 1960s or 1970s. Their accounts and experiences were glaringly absent from most journalistic, political or literary material of that time, yet my academic supervisor nonetheless asked me to visit archives and include what I found there in my work.

Sitting in record offices around West Yorkshire, I found pamphlets, newspaper clippings, sociological reports and health resources that repeatedly narrated the women that I was speaking to as unintelligent, unhygienic and lacking at every level. I was supposed to use these documents as references even though they never included the voices of the women themselves. They were a record of nothing more than the projection of tropes that aimed to re-emphasise the greatness of the real subject of the archive: Whiteness.

I wonder what myriad of things *we don't know we don't know*. And I wonder how the erasure of their erasure means that we castigate many of the final witnesses to historic violence as crazy, ill or unreliable.

Although my nineteen white IKEA boxes are full of things that seem useless and banal, and I sometimes wonder when or why I would ever look at them again, their presence is a testimony, even if I never re-open those boxes.

THAT DAY

AFTER MUNEERA PILGRIM[5]

I think of the stories the earth will tell on the day she unloads
   her weight
discharges her burdens[6]   وَأَخْرَجَتِ ٱلْأَرْضُ أَثْقَالَهَا
the day she relates her news[7]   يَوْمَئِذٍ تُحَدِّثُ أَخْبَارَهَا

What will she report of the heaviness buried in her oceans?
What will she tell of the weighted crates stacked with
   evidence?
What will she say of the bodies?

On that day when the depths of the earth are discharged
and humankind says,   وَقَالَ ٱلْإِنسَٰنُ مَا لَهَا
   'what is wrong with her?'[8]

What will those who packed the boxes have to say?
What will those who marked the papers think?
What will the ship crews have left to feel inside their chests?

And when the ashes are gathered back together
and the books rebound
no wonder that will be the day of Account

I worry about my memory. I seem to forget things almost as soon as I absorb them. It sometimes makes me feel my skin has no inside. My mum says it's because I've spent too long remembering difficult things. I think she is overly empathetic. I would say I have spent more time emptying difficult things out of my brain. Careful to write everything down so I do not have to hold it. The white boxes speak for themselves.

As early as primary school, I remember Mrs Bateman telling us to write a list before bed. *It helps you sleep*, she said. I have always slept well (praise be to Allah), but the problem now is that everything is on paper and nothing in my head. I sift through old journals to recall who my friends were. Did I go anywhere in the summer of 2010? What were my hobbies? Let me go read up on myself.

In language lessons I am confident with grammatical breakdowns but cannot keep up with speaking and listening. Vocabulary enters my ears, then gets stuck waiting for direction. Without a pen in hand, I feel useless.

My mother remembers more about my life than I do. She recounts anecdotes I have told her, and I laugh in surprise on hearing them. Did that really happen to me? Did I tell you that? I find myself advising friends to watch films they recommended to me the week before. I view the same TV shows repeatedly because I cannot remember their twists.

This all seems rather funny, and it would be. But recently, scrolling through my open internet tabs, I found a search for *memory recall issues in your 20s* and paused to ponder how seriously I feel this relates to me.

They say trauma affects the memory in multiple ways, often distorting, disorganising or fragmenting it. A body coping with trauma can even block out memories altogether. Sometimes, a person is unable to remember important information about their own life—events that took place, or their very identity.

Psychologists call this dissociative amnesia and have linked the condition to overwhelming stress caused by major trauma. I think about how my grandmother says she remembers nothing of her life prior to migration, despite being twenty-eight when she came to England. When I ask about her wedding day, she tells me she does not remember.

I am twenty-eight now, too, and my memory of my own life is already patchy. Whenever I test out my theory about this on friends, I use a joking voice to downplay my concern. *I don't remember much of my time studying at Cambridge in detail*, I smile, *maybe because it was so traumatic, right?* They laugh along. But when I attempt to retrieve a memory from my early twenties, I feel as though I am wading through thick mud. Afraid of losing my way, I turn back. Once when I opened a journal from my first year of university, I found I could not bear to read beyond a few sides. I put it back in the box and let those pages remain the last conscious witness.

When I speak on a panel at an event about oral histories, a young man asks me how we can go about recording our elders' stories when they avoid our questions. I do not have a good answer for him, because trauma has long and winding arms that a voice-recording app cannot always surmount. Perhaps our elders truly don't remember. Perhaps not remembering is the best way for them to survive. I understand that this makes record-making and accountability-seeking difficult. But unless we can offer alternatives for how to survive pain, who are we to ask our elders to excavate it for the sake of record-keeping?

Besides, the mere fact of not being verbalised doesn't mean a memory has been erased. Although my grandmother denies remembering her life in Pakistan, when I travel with her to the town where she was born, her feet have no difficulty recalling the streets. Google Maps gives no road names, but she leads me with confidence, her footsteps revealing the aliveness of her recollections, even if she cannot articulate them. She remembers, and she is remembered.

To counter Google, I mark every house we stop at on my Maps app and name it specifically: 'house of the cousin with three ducks', 'house aunty Razia grew up in and kids moved back', 'Uncle dispute land'. Nani finds such note-taking and the accompanying photography preposterous. She chides me for my constant journaling, but I manage to fill three 200-page notebooks in three months. I carry them home in my hand luggage in case anything happens to my checked-in baggage. The thought alone is too much to consider.

On the slowest days, Nani asks what even happened for me to write about. Perhaps my over-memorialising seems as strange to her as her non-remembering seems to me. But in some ways, they each require one another. The deafening silence of her memory makes me desperate to archive, and my recordings take the pressure off her silence.

And maybe, ironically, my poor memory of my own life is what drives me to memorialise hers. As terrible as I am with my own recollections, I have made sure to know my grandparents' memories well, like dhikr beads worn by the grooves of fingers that hold them often. Since my teenage years, I have compiled notes, family trees, voice recordings and videos of my grand-parents, and even more besides. All sit inside my IKEA boxes.

I wonder sometimes if my nineteen white boxes are an attempt at defensive resistance. An effort to build a back-story, a history, a fortress in the face of erased erasure. To be seen, or if not to be seen, to make my not being seen felt.

I want the kind of history that can't be told in classrooms / That can't be told in English / That can't be told, only known / That is knowledge only in the sense that it is known / I want knowledge that is unrecognisable / I want unrecognisable histories / Histories that oar through the mouths of languages they didn't make into data sets / I want the kind of history that cannot become a data set / History that makes a mess out of the spreadsheet / History that messes with the future, messes with the present, messes with yesterday / History that makes you breathless, swings you by your feet, licks your face completely inappropriately, jumps out from behind the thing called history and doesn't say 'boo' because it's not a ghost / I want the kind of history that old men with dementia can tell you and if you listened every day you might think was always the same story / I want the kind of history that is never the same story because no version is the only version / I want the version that is half imagined / I want the memory that you can no longer distinguish from dream or reality / I want dreamy reality / I want dreams that are real / I want oral sources that still speak to me / I want to slurp up the archives and write a musical about what we find but then ban the music as impermissible, humiliating the institution, refuse to sell tickets to the target audience / I want a play that nobody watches, that kind of history, a regret for the Arts Council / I want the kind of history that can't be held on to / The kind of history you dream of / The kind of history that makes you travel the world just to try on its shoes / I want that kind of history

ג

BECOMING A SIGHT / THE PORTAL OF OBJECTHOOD

ACT I: SCENE II

the writer and *the book* *stand opposite each other, mirroring one another. If either one has a body distinct from the other, we cannot tell. They are in a beautiful public library that is dissolving around them. Time is a metaphor of dappled light coming through a window in the ceiling and **her fear** is the shadow between every beam of light.*

her fear *is sensed by the writer and the book but not heard. As a result, they speak over her.*

(Overlapping speech is indicated by forward slashes.)

the writer	You're not what I thought you were /going to be/
her fear	/You're not/ /good enough/
the book	/What did you/ /expect?/
her fear	/I need/ /them to understand! Don't you know that?/
the writer	/You were supposed to be about seeing/ and being seen About the different gazes upon us and how to see ourselves without them

the book *looks smirkingly at the writer, knowing more than her (as always).*

the book	Is that not what I am?
the writer	Well, it's just you seem more preoccupied with what *I* am

than with being what I want you to be

*Pause. The audience should suddenly become aware that **her eyes**, **her heart**, **her head** and **her soul** are also privy to the scene—they are floating in the water that the library is becoming.*

the book   Is that so different from what you expected?

***the writer** and **the book** stare at each other for a long time. Eventually, **her head** cannot hold her tongue.*

her head   Of course it is!

her heart   But, maybe that's okay?

her fear   It's not okay!
Stop ignoring me!
But don't look at me either!

***her eyes** close and **the writer** subtly pushes **her fear** out of the library, locking the doors. **the book** shakes its head, knowing more than her (as always).*

the book   You'll have to let her in at some point, you
know ...

***her head** momentarily slips under the water from shock, whilst **her heart** sorrowfully looks toward the locked doors. **her eyes** stay closed to give **the writer** and **the book** a moment together. **the writer** should try to remain unmoved.*

When my grandparents crossed this border, they were trans-formed from subjects into objects. From Ahmed and Surriya, the best volleyball player in the village and the most fragrant of the trio of sisters in the town, to just a couple of immigrants. A state-conferred status meaning thing, unseen, crawling between factory and terraced house.

Not only in and of themselves were they robbed of subject-hood, but also in relation to others. I imagine my grandpar-ents arriving at the British border with dozens of titles in tow, symbolising bonds of love, blood and care. My grandmother as a vadi phen (an eldest sister), a bhau (a daughter-in-law), biwi (wife), deverani (younger brother's wife), saali (wife's sister), pateeji (niece on the brother's side), bhanji (niece on the sister's side), massi (mother's-side auntie or second cousin), phuphi (father's-side auntie or second cousin), ma (mother), sutee-li-bhen (step-sister via her father's side), dhotri (granddaughter on her mother's side), potri (granddaughter on her father's side), and more. But when they exited the plane at Heathrow, every epithet vanished into the portal of objecthood—tossed away, irrelevant. New names were prescribed: Asian mother, black immigrant, Indian, thing, it.

Once, when I was performing in Halifax, a woman named Salihah translated one of my poems into Pothwari. Where I had written, 'Muslim women are perceived only as objects,' she elaborated through her interpretation, 'musalman aurat ek cheez eh, jestran koi table eh ya koi glass eh'. A Muslim woman is a thing, like a table, or a glass.

The immediacy of the comparison shocked me, even though that is precisely what objectification means. Robin Wall Kimmerer, a member of the Potawatomi tribe of the Great Lakes region of the colonised lands of North America, writes about this too. She explains that while non-human beings are denoted in English by the pronoun 'it' and thus differentiated

SEEING FOR OURSELVES

from humans, Indigenous languages do not create these same distinctions.[1] She looks primarily at how objectifying language impacts human relationships with nature, asking what would happen if we saw a tree, for example, as a fellow living being rather than as an 'it'.

But when we consider that alongside the categorisation of the 'natural world' into classes of objects of study and organisation, Europe's Enlightenment thinkers also ranked people in hierarchies determined by 'race' (which was claimed to be a 'natural' reality too), it's clear that languages like English don't just distinguish between humans and non-humans to determine what is an 'it'. We non-white/non-European humans have longed been marked as 'its' too.

What does it mean to be an 'it'? To be made into ek cheez, like a table or a glass, and perhaps even lesser? What does that do to you?

My grandmother used to knit cardigans for the Jonathan Silver menswear chain in 1970s Bradford. Some winters ago, she tasked me with the challenge of learning to knit too. I saw it as a chance to emulate some of the skills she had, so I was happy when she asked me to begin by reading a knitting pattern to her. However, shame quickly engulfed me as I stumbled and stuttered over what I read.

'How many rows to start? Knit or purl?' Nani asked. I could not make sense of the pattern, with all its abbreviations, brackets and numbers. My fluent English tongue waved like an embarrassingly loud flag in the waters of my mouth. I told her I would take the pattern home and figure it out.

After hours spent hunched over YouTube, I began knitting a single sleeve. I knitted for almost a week until, nearing completion, I realised I had followed the pattern incorrectly and the sleeve was half as wide as it should have been. When I showed Nani, she just shrugged: *these things happen*. Without hesitation, she unravelled the entire yarn.

Crushed but unrelenting, I began again. It took me a month in total, and bear in mind that Nani had already knitted the back of the cardigan some years before. But eventually, I arrived at her house with a gift bag and new set of skills. She took the cardigan out, looked over the cable-knit front that I had astounded myself making, her expression unreadable, and eventually patted the piece, saying it was all right. I had never felt prouder.

In the 1970s, Nani recalls, she was paid around five pounds per cardigan that she knitted. My mother used to walk past Jonathan Silver as a girl and see those same mohair cardigans sell for almost eighty pounds. As Nani stepped off that plane at Heathrow, the portal of objecthood transfigured her into units of economic value that did not even approach the value of the products of her labour. What does it mean to be worth less than the yarn knotted together by your own fingers?

*

My grandfather repeatedly tells a story about his first job in Bradford in 1961. The factory boss asked if he could spin cotton. Nana said he couldn't, but he was willing to learn. Very soon he was put in charge of multiple machines, a point of much pride for him.

As we are all familiar with by now, the main reason most of the UK's textiles today are imported and no longer made domestically is that it is cheaper that way. The hands that make our cloth, that make our clothes, that sew and knit and hem and embroider and spin and stain and dye and fasten and button and zip and thread, are hands we consider less valuable than the hands of 'British workers'. Before the UK outsourced this labour overseas, the same principle was applied to immigrant workers, who were understood to be a better option than non-migrants to employ in the textile mills of industrial regions like Yorkshire. You could pay them less, for more.

At six foot three or four, Nana was the tallest man in his village, much like his nana. As such, he was the best volleyball player in the village too—I find it hard to picture him jumping up and down, lungi hitched around his waist. He tells us he was misbehaved at school but that he used to sing. Music has remained an abiding love of his. Even whilst many things escape him now, a familiar qawwali can root him.

Sometimes, as I sit with my grandparents, I wonder whether they felt the objecthood imposed on them through the portal of the border in one fell swoop or over years. There is no question that accounts for what I wish to know, so instead of asking about it, I observe them, as I often have done.

It occurs to me that perhaps I am not seeking an answer to that question at all; perhaps I am just trying to see them truly and deeply, because it is the oversight of them as seeable that is the theft from them that I grieve the most. Or, if I am more honest, it is the theft from them that most seeps into my own longing to be seen. A longing that, after many months of sitting with them, I realise they might not actually share.

I am stunned viscerally by this realisation when I watch Nani cook. Nobody who has eaten her food would contradict the statement that Nani has barakah in her hands. Blessings. Whatever she makes, even if you have followed the same recipe, is simply in a different category of taste from what you've had before.

One day, I delve into this with her. I say that, if you think about it, the barakah in her hands extends to the innumerable skills she has embodied through them—knitting, sewing, embroidering, cooking, and all the labour of love, care and child-rearing—masha Allah, it was Allah's will. The day her hands speak for her, I cannot imagine how much they will have to say. How much good they have sent forth—may Allah accept it, ameen.

When I think this aloud, Nani listens with a quiet confidence. There is something in the way she listens that makes me realise my naivety. She has already known this; she has always been privy to her own skills and complexity. I am suddenly embarrassed by the arrogance of my assumption that I am doing her a favour in seeing her. She never needed me to. Instead, I realise that my desire to see and document her and Nana so deeply and closely is actually a desire to see myself in context. To see myself more fully than a history mutated by the portal of the border would allow.

Perhaps I was alone in finding the idea of losing boxes filled with scraps of paper or photographs too much to consider, then. For how much more have they been forced to bear, and how much more unseen have they been? Could it be that they aren't preoccupied with the questions that preoccupy me because they learnt to see themselves somewhere before being tossed through the portal of the border? I, by contrast, do not recall a life before objecthood. What a strange possibility: not to consider yourself strange.

The unique Western-ness of the experience of not knowing ourselves before we were objects has often become most clear to me when I have made friends who grew up in South Asian or African countries and moved to the West in adulthood. They all relate similar confusion. Going to the countryside and being treated with 'unexplainable' disdain. 'Random' acts of intolerance or inconsistency from a shopkeeper, or a landlord, or an academic. It is the predicament of having passed through the portal of objecthood without understanding that they have become sights. This causes problems. A sight that thinks itself seeing is intolerable, oxymoronic.

In contrast, we natives of the West learnt to internalise the eye from the moment we left the womb, the last place where we weren't strangers.[2] We know we are sights even better than those who see us do. For example, most Muslims are more fluent in what things are seen as 'signs of radicalisation' than those who are told to look out for their appearance in us. A woman tells me she wears pastel-coloured hijabs to work so as not to frighten her colleagues. A lecturer tells me he taught a course on Islam to the Ministry of Defence to demonstrate its suitability for the university curriculum.

We are the pre-emptive eye inside ourselves. We are the thought police before the action is formed. We are the portal into which we throw ourselves and each other.

But what is a portal to objecthood if not a black hole? And how many times can a black hole disappear inside itself before it cataclysmically implodes?

Some days, even still, I naively feel myself attempt to usurp my objecthood. Sometimes, a laugh will rise to my lips that is not my own. A pacification laugh. It comes on suddenly and catches me off guard. Nobody notices but me. It multiplies my horror that it can happen even after all these years of refutation and research.

Last year, I attended the ninetieth birthday of a white woman, a friend I had volunteered with a decade or more ago. I knew what the demographic of her street, the neighbourhood and thus the party would be. I am fluent in the ways of such demographics; I live amongst them. So, I braced myself and attended.

Although I was welcomed with warmth, I was also aware, so very aware, of the ease with which my limbs kicked into an auto-pilot mode that I had not experienced for several years during the pandemic. I moved in a way that was disarming, making obscenely easy jokes as one who had studied the preferred wit of the white middle classes might. I was self-deprecating. I made references or alluded to them with surprising muscle memory.

I was simultaneously inside and outside myself. Ashamed and amazed. Performance would be the wrong word; it was more possession. Something taking me over, something learned, responsive and bizarre.

When I recounted this to somebody I had just met in a writing workshop, he said, 'It's funny you think of it like that. I call that my trauma response. I call that survival.' Whilst I believe he is right to see this as a learned response to the surveillance and disciplining of the white gaze, there is still a part of me that knows it is not only fear that's at work but also seduction. To make yourself palatable to the white gaze is not only demanded—it is incentivised. The more acceptable you are, the more you're rewarded, socially, culturally, economically.

When I perform the Palatable Disembodied Muslim, even despite myself, I know it comes partly from a desire not to feel pain or punishment, but it also comes from a desire to be approved. The seductiveness of the white gaze hangs thick in the air like a heavy fog, obscuring and inescapable.

Before her death, my friend Dr Azeezat Johnson and I would discuss how, as girls, we attempted to transcend our bodies by drawing attention to the 'goodness' of our minds. Knowing that our ability to succeed in the school exam system was rewardable but that our racialised bodies were not, we hoped the latter might be overlooked in favour of our minds. This disembodiment, learnt at so young an age, is hard to unlearn. So we tried now to give our bodies attention and time, to treat them (ourselves) with compassion rather than as obstacles to overcome in order for us to be seen. And that is the central contradiction: the attempt to be seen as individual, valuable and commendable comes at the price of disappearing and over-looking our bodies as gendered and racialised chores.

Perhaps this is why I came home so tired after the ninetieth birthday party. Being able to disembody myself at such short notice, in an instant, remains frightening and exhausting. More troubling is seeing how immediately it is rewarded but simultaneously knowing how conditional that reward is, how it does not keep me safe.

I recall doing a similar disembodied dance at a 'street party' on the road my grandparents had recently moved to. I chatted in the courteous, distant-yet-familiar way that I know is correct and asked all the questions you are supposed to. But I found myself caught out when a neighbour brought up the matter of the United States' recent withdrawal from Afghanistan, which had been all over the news that summer. She worriedly remarked that the fate of young girls and women would now be miserable.

I was slammed back into my body with sudden force. I knew somehow that it (I) was tied to the fictive fates of the girls and women in the conversation, and so I tried to intervene quickly, without over-complicating my thought. I said something simple but—I hoped—provocative, a question as to whether we could assume the fate of women and girls under US military occupation had been ideal.

But as the words left my mouth and suffused the air of the street, I knew that they were the wrong density to sit unnoticed in the fog. They cast a shadow. A shadow suggesting I was not who I seemed. Despite the act I'd been putting on, I was who they had known me to be all along.

I left the conversation politely, wishing ardently that geopolitics had never come up. I began making a mental list of safe topics that would leave me disembodied and floating in the future. But there are none. Because disembodied floating can never be safety. Disembodied floating means existing only in the black hole that is the portal. And that is no place to live.

HER

AFTER JOELLE TAYLOR[3]

When they search her they are showing her herself
These are your eyes, wandering
dangerously ungrateful
repressed at best, treacherous at worst

Here is your translucent skeleton
your threateningly reproductive skull

They lay out her teeth on the table
can these be inverted somehow?
so they no longer gnash but smile in acquiescence?

Her hands are splayed flat before them
too much like prayer
they show her how to close them like gatekeeping

The last part of her body that they show her is not part of it at all
they say this is most vital
touch it only with metallic tools
specimen sample
we know how volatile these can be
saw them on the Durand Line
or worse, didn't

Do you know what happens to things we can't see?
a siren blares
flashing lights rove

This is unacceptable

NOTHING CAN PUT YOU OFF DOING A PHD LIKE ATTENDING ACADEMIC CONFERENCES

I sit in a room that is ostensibly circular but feels perpendicular. Everybody talks about Muslims. First a white man. Then a white man. Their work looks at Muslims. Not looking *with* us. Not looking at *themselves*. But looking *at us*.

My pink hijab is luminous in this room. Things start unravelling absurdly when it becomes clear we are not, in fact, 'all on the same page'. Two former counter-terrorism policemen happen to be sitting to my left, and after lunch a white male academic disparages the notion of boycotts. How will policy ever be changed if we don't sit at the table and have a voice? It's juvenile!

My heart pounds. My hand is in the air. I am speaking. I cannot manage the politeness that a diplomatic space such as this requires. I am uncivil. I breathlessly proclaim that it's wrong to assume boycotts hope for the same kind of change that policymaking aims for. Some of us don't set our sights on piecemeal reforms. Some of us can't legitimise a room in which there are people who want to strip us of our citizenships or detain us without charge. I am not willing to sit at a table where my humanity is in question. And besides, the table exists not because the case against it has not been made, but because it has beneficiaries.

The table is a box of the worst kind: the table is a cage.

The room is silent. The air is filled with cracks. After a moment, the white academic says, 'I take your point.' The room is silent once more. The cracks threaten to split the air open. My heart is loud in my head. I am holding my own hand to still the shaking.

Later, he approaches me to say I am eloquent. It is always this way. I should say he is condescending. But instead, I say something like, I hope you understand I'm just passionate about this topic, that's all. As though 'this topic' is a pastime, not my humanity.

I feel sick to my stomach when I perform to the room. I am not nervous, but there is something sterile about the gaze of academics that does not exist in other rooms where I perform. I look over everybody's heads.

The chair of the event says that today the use of the word 'racist' will be applauded, that this is a novel kind of academic space. But the word sits heavy on my tongue. The word sits expectant at the door of the room. You can only enter academic spaces with a key-card these days. I think of my friend buried by academia. I think of how a room cannot rely on the subjects of the research, hearts pounding, to be their saving grace.

I make a mental note to self: withdraw consent from participating in academic conferences in future. The table is a cage.

HIM

AFTER JOELLE TAYLOR

When they search him they are showing him himself
This is your beard
length of a fist
a punching fist only, of course

Here is your mixed-metaphor body
your calligraphy skin

The only imagery I remember to make of him is sirens and
   police cars
the security state has hampered my creativity
all I can see to make a motif of you is marching boots,
   truncheons, officers

The last part of his body that they show him is his tongue
they say, we know these
what these are used for
what your people do with these
seen them in Afghanistan
saw them back in the Orient
seen what they do to language
turn it to sehr
سحر
magic
bad magic
black magic
not magic like theirs which is
white

the magic to disappear, erase, forget, pretend
magic to make you small
magic to make the possible appear
distant

A white friend of mine—at least then if not now—once remarked (intending, I am sure, to be tongue in cheek) that if he were ever asked whether he had seen any early warning signs of my radicalisation, he would have to concede that yes, he had. This was said in the context of our being undergraduate students at the University of Cambridge, and probably of my doing something like refusing to kneel before the college 'master', or referring to the university as foundationally white supremacist because of its investments, endowments and ideological knowledge production.[4]

I doubt my friend would recall his comment now, but I think about that exchange a lot. There have been two or three specific moments in my life when I have recognised deep within myself that I am exactly the sight to be seen and sorted that the British Transport Police, or the government, urge you to look out for.

I remember once being on the train between Bradford and Leeds. The blue-and-purple pattern of Northern Rail is woven into the fibre of this memory. I watched Yorkshire fields through the window and felt the sensation of a barricade erecting itself along my skin, through the air, as the 'See It, Say It, Sorted' announcement was made. The sharpness of the sensation was indicative of the fact that I was precisely the thing to be feared.

I felt a sudden certainty in the knowledge that *of course* I required surveillance, because in truth there was nothing that made more sense to me than the destruction of the state's endlessly violent arms. I saw within myself that I had no real qualms about armed resistance to this state and its brutalising institutions, which cause needless suffering and misery to so many so daily. And, as if floating above the train carriage, I saw that this line of thinking was totally reasonable yet simultaneously the cause of my utter impossibility as a subject of reason. I could now only be an object of suspicion.

I wrote a quick note on my phone at the time:

It is 9pm on the train back from Bradford when it hits me / I am radical / Of course I am / I am vehemently outraged by the violence of this state / I am consumed with fury when I consider the mutilation of lives and humanity /

Does it make my bones criminal that they cannot stand still under my skin when the world is burning? / Does it make my voice dangerous that my tongue cannot lie flat when the world is screaming? / I'd rather be radical than grasping for limper labels to be thrown like scraps my way

My friend, who had predicted this 'radicalisation' as a joke, had unwittingly accurately referred to the impact that attending an elite academic institution had had on me. As I retorted at the time, the only thing that had radicalised me was seeing, up close, how white supremacy operates at a structural level, and the impossibility of ending it without dramatic rupture. However many 'diverse' faces might fill its halls and surround its tables, the processes of the institution were historically hardwired to uphold white Eurocentric hierarchies of knowing and valuation.

It was at Cambridge that I learnt for the first time that a table carved from human remains cannot be reformed, and that if we want to build a just world, some things must simply be destroyed. And it was only on the 9 p.m. train from Bradford that I realised this knowledge made my brain a threat.

*

The second moment in my life when I recall a similarly specific dissociative realisation was late on a Friday night. I had been let into the headquarters of one of the world's largest news media broadcasters to wait for a friend. My bag was checked upon my entry, as was my person. Satisfied that I did not pose an imminent security risk, the security staff left me to sit upstairs with a visitor's badge and some peppermint tea.

The building was quiet, practically empty. I was sleepy and ponderous, and in a haze of lazy associations, I thought, almost without thinking, about how possible it would be to set off a fire alarm to have the building evacuated and, once it was empty, to detonate it to the ground. No one would be hurt, but the symbolic and actual destruction of a narrative arm of Western imperialism would be powerful.

And then I realised that as much as that act made political sense, it would be completely pointless for me to do it, because my motivation would be erased and re-written as senseless violence, cultural violence, religious violence, fanatical violence. The act of revolutionary property destruction of the mouthpiece of global capitalism would not be noted. My intentions would be irrelevant and my act depoliticised. I took another sip of peppermint tea and settled into my seat to wait.

*

And now, as I write this, I am engaged in perhaps the third of these specific moments of realisation. I am thinking about the hundreds who have been charged and convicted under Section 58 of the Terrorism Act 2000,[5] which makes it a criminal offence to collect, make, possess or—ever since an amendment in 2019—view online[6] a document containing information that could 'be useful to a person committing or preparing an act of terrorism'. Crucially, no proof of intent for use is required. Under TACT 2000, Muslims have been detained for merely downloading files to their computers and convicted for owning magazines.[7]

I am thinking about how typing the words above marks me as a dangerous object. There is no other way to read me. I am something to be watched, to be kept within view.

There is a circular irony to this, because I wonder if it is the very pre-emption of my apparent potential for violence that has enabled me to imagine it myself. Learning to look at yourself as a probable enactor of future violence makes things you might

49

not have previously considered feel more and more possible, at least to imagine, at least to play out in the mind's eye. For it is not the acting that we are concerned about in our present moment or in the law—it is the thought. To think of resistance, as a non-state actor, is already to be dangerous. Already criminal.

Which is amusing, no? For would I feel such concern about writing these paragraphs if I were writing about my desire to become a policeman? Or a desire to join the military and kill Arabs abroad? Would I be deemed a threat or a danger then? What if I wrote about lazily imagining myself as a G4S guard cuffing an asylum-seeking person to board them onto a chartered deportation flight? What if I wrote about one day realising how much this seemed like a viable thing for me to do? That would merely be career progress; that would be aspirational. 'Good on the girl! She's defied her inner propensity for violence!' they'd say. 'What a hero!'

*

The day I first draft this essay, I receive an email from a journalist asking me for comment on a piece in which he will write that I have performed and worked alongside people he deems problematic because of their commitment to liberating Palestine from settler-colonialism. There is little to nothing about me in the email, nor much about anything I have said or done.

I understand the threat is not in what he will write about me but in how he can manoeuvre and distort a gaze upon me. There is nothing I can do but wait for the swell of a tide of fear as I am made into a dangerous object, an object to distance oneself from.

I go for a long walk and buy a soft-scoop ice cream with a Flake that begins to melt too soon. I think about how strange it is to feel so small and yet be made out to be so threatening. I think about how there must be something threatening for the silencing to be sought in the first place. I think about what types of ostracism and alienation lead people to participate in armed struggle to begin with. I think about how difficult armed struggle must be when unarmed struggle is made so wearisome. I finish my ice cream and walk home, a thing, ek cheez, crawling between park and terraced house.

۴

STRIVING TO SEE /
SEEKING SUBJECTHOOD
IS A CIRCLE

In April 2018 I was invited to perform my poetry in Las Vegas. I had spent the previous three months in Pakistan and flown back to the UK for only a few days' interim, so in Vegas, where the night and day seemed to merge into one, I found myself missing Pakistan's five calls to prayer a day from a multitude of adhans. On the Friday of my stay, I vividly recall reading Surat al-Kahf whilst sitting on the famous Vegas Strip. Muslims are encouraged to read this chapter of the Quran on Fridays to receive illumination in the coming week. I searched for luminosity from the heavens amidst glaring neon signs.

On the afternoon of one of my performances, we prepared ourselves backstage in a room usually used for cabaret. Behind the curtains there was a gigantic martini glass used by burlesque dancers. The thought of climbing into it momentarily entered my head; I didn't, though I have often wondered what makes something a performance. Sometimes, the only thing that feels different about being on stage is having consented to the eyes on me. Behind the curtain and in front of the curtain. Inside your head and aloud. The lines between these things are unfixed.

In my first one-woman poetry show later that year, I opened with a piece reflecting on this:

I am not a performer / this is not a show / you will not be entertained today / I am not a performer / this is not a stage / you will not applaud my hurt today / Because I am a daily spectacle / walking, always on show / the critics laud, applaud, jeer and condemn / you watch me daily on your screens already / review my pain and body by the load / So this is not creative / this is not a show / Or if it is, it's because I already am through no choice of my own / But I am not performing / Because I am not a performer

Curating a 'self' for the stage and simultaneously wanting the audience to realise that it is not distinct from the self that you're forced to curate daily is complicated. I have mixed feelings about the visibility I experience standing on stages, reading my poems or giving talks. Some days, it has enabled me to feel I can resist being collapsed into the nothingness that the media would have me be, because instead I get to be listened to. In those moments, I feel a fire inside me and an ability to speak with defiance I cannot muster elsewhere. But other times, it is the opposite. No matter how much or how loudly I speak, I know I am not being seen or heard for myself. Even as I perform, I see a glossy coat of white mist obscure the eyes of those who watch me. The 'real' me is impossible to see behind the lenses through which they look at me. That feeling is intolerable.

So, in 2021, when my friend Alaa Alsaraji asked me to tell her about a space I felt safe in, I thought of the place where I felt most free from others' eyes. Alaa is a visual artist and was working on a project called *Mapping Sanctuaries*, for which she interviewed Muslims about where we felt safety and belonging and illustrated the places we described.[1] I remember the embarrassment I felt when I saw her exhibition in its totality. I feel it again now just recollecting this. Every other piece depicted somewhere communal, with titles like *Green Street*, *Whitechapel*, *Uxbridge Road*, *Manchester Art Gallery* and *Mother's Living Room*.

Mine was called *My Bedroom*.

By naming my bedroom as my sanctuary, I had suggested that my sense of safety relied on the absence of other people. This embarrassed me because I do not believe it to be true, politically speaking. I frequently argue that our well-being depends on communal care and interdependence. And yet, there is obviously a conflicting part of me that does not quite *feel* this. A part of me that experiences safety as solitude. Perhaps this is because when I am alone, I am safe from being read, perceived, misunderstood. Alone, I am certain I am not an object. I am not an 'it'. I do not have to perform. I am safe from the sight of others.

When I told a friend about my choice of sanctuary and shared my speculations about what was behind it, they were somewhat affronted. They asked if this meant that I am not being myself when I am with people. This was a strange conclusion. I am always being myself, but I am rarely the *entirety* of myself. Who of us is? We all wear masks of one kind or another, because the very fact of being witnessed impacts the ways we are ourselves. And for those of us made hyper-visible by legislators and journalists, our masking is even more coercively demanded. A sanctuary is exactly what I crave sometimes. A place to be cut off from the gazes and mores of society. A place to be *all of me,* even if the price is solitude.

Maybe this also underpins some of my anxieties about this book. For although my aspiration is for this to be a place where I can be *all of me,* I cannot pretend I am entirely alone here because I know that eventually you will read me. A true sanctuary would need to be unreachable, like a hidden cave.

The name of the surah I read in Vegas that Friday, al-Kahf, means 'The Cave'. It tells the story of a group of youths fleeing a society where they are at risk of persecution because of their monotheism. They are instructed to take refuge in a cave, where God enables them to sleep for hundreds of years without being found, until, when He awakes them, the surrounding society and its norms have changed.

A cave is what I desire. I think of the cave of Hira, where the Prophet Muhammad ﷺ would go into seclusion for long periods of devotion and prayer. It was here that he first received Allah's revelation from the Angel Jibril (or Gabriel).

Caves have long been a motif of solitude, spiritual awakening and mysticism. A well-known cave of a different kind is the one from Plato's allegory in *The Republic*. In this cave, a group of people is chained so they can only see the cave's back wall. Behind them is a fire which casts onto the wall shadows of objects and puppets that people walking outside the cave carry past its mouth. The chained people assume that the shadows constitute reality, although they are merely fragments of the things they represent. Plato argues that in our lives, most of us stay inside the cave, convinced by the shadow-reality of things, never entering the light.

In the eleventh century, Imam al-Ghazali, one of the most influential and prominent scholars in Islamic history, offered a different analysis. For al-Ghazali, if the cave represents a false reality, then staying inside the cave is a metaphor for life in this world. True reality cannot be perceived in our lifetimes, because it only opens to us when we leave this world. Only at death are the veils to the light of reality lifted.

Many more knowledgeable than me have written about the allegory of the cave in the history of thought. I am neither a philosopher nor a scholar, so I have little to offer in that regard, but as a poet I find my mind wants to take these metaphors elsewhere. What happens when *we* are the realities that pass across the mouth of the cave, and all that the world sees of us are our shadows? And what about when we are forced to succumb to society's false belief that we are only shadows, despite knowing the truth that we are more? And what if the cave is the place where we go to stop performing, but as a result, we go unseen? Is it preferable to be alone and unseen or to be amongst others but seen only as a shadow?

And further, what happens when we go to the cave to seek refuge but find ourselves diverted to debating the reality of shadows with the people who are already inside? Is it preferable to face persecution by the shadow-gazing society because we refuse to accept that the shadow is all that we are? Or to sit in shackles and stare at the wall in a semblance of safety?

READING SURAT AL-KAHF
ON THE LAS VEGAS STRIP

إِنَّا جَعَلْنَا مَا عَلَى ٱلْأَرْضِ زِينَةً لَّهَا لِنَبْلُوَهُمْ أَيُّهُمْ أَحْسَنُ عَمَلًا

Indeed, We have made that which is on the earth adornment for
it in order that We may test them [as to] which of them is best
in deed.[2]

The pomp and glitter of this life
does not look so tempting up close as you might think
has a bad smell and no daylight
and though I do not know what heaven looks like
I'd wager it's the inverse
of artificial fountains in the Nevada desert
coerced Zamzams backed by neon lights

This is neither a garden owned by a man who is grateful
nor a garden owned by a man who is ungrateful
this is a garden dried to ash
owned by a man asleep in a cave, not sure how much time
     has passed

and when awoken
he thinks the cave is the beginning and end of it all
gazing up at a painted sky on a gaudy roof
unaware of a world of brighter hues

If this is the pomp and glitter
it's the kind that only looks good in a certain light
by the morning it makes your eyelids itch
stands as a reminder to the tragedy of the night before
the tragedy of the life before

the lesser life

REPRESENTATION IS
SHADOW PUPPETRY
AT ITS BEST

In a world bent on celebrating 'representation', we are made to applaud shadows because they vaguely share our outlines, whilst we are left choking on toxic fumes and ignoring those who pull the puppet strings. It is the pinnacle of performativity. Yet if any critique of representation is made, it tends to revolve around how there is not enough of it, or how to 'really' be representative. Generalisations are berated for disappearing our differences, and specificities are rebuked for leaving too many of us out. In this unwinnable back-and-forth, the end goal of representation remains ambiguous.

In the mainstream, presence itself is deemed the good. To be at the table, lauded. First prime minister of South Asian heritage, first shalwar kameez in the House of Lords, first woman of colour in charge of deportations. We're told it symbolises something. But what? What does it symbolise specifically? If it shows anything incredible about institutions, it is their malleability to absorb and co-opt difference and resistance, not their ability to change. Inclusion becomes a swallowing into the same intestine, not a transformation of the digestive process: the filthy outcome is unaltered. *We* are transformed whilst the institution is unaffected beyond the surface level. Sure, there may be some unease, a turned-up nose, but is that the objective? If the people of colour on the streets, the women in shalwar kameez at the border, still experience inhumanity in every aspect of social and political life, then what was the purpose?

Still, ever keen to be 'represented', we fold ourselves into pre-packaged boxes: nations, ethnicities and B-A-M-E, a ragbag label made up of a colour (Black), a continent (Asian) and a societal proportion (Minority Ethnic). Everybody knows it makes no sense. Everybody grumbles. Everybody resents the equality and diversity monitoring forms we're asked to fill in. But our complaints are that they discredit our hopeful performances of belonging ('Why can you only be White-British and not Black-British?!'), or that they overgeneralise ('What is Asian "Other"?!' 'Why can't you be "Mixed" with two non-White parents?!'). Such questions rightly reveal the absurdity of demographic data sets, but they stop short of rejecting the categories because *they make us*, full-stop.

Rarely do we resent that we find ourselves clinging on to the same bounded taxonomies that were imposed on us to divide and contain us in the first place. Instead, because we want the shadows to look 'more like us', we end up exaggerating our own edges, making caricatures of ourselves in the hope that what is cast onto the wall is closer to what we 'are'. But as all puppet masters know, this is merely negotiating with illusions. And as all firefighters know, there is no negotiation with fire. No matter the shape or specificity of the puppet, the shadow depends on the way the puppet is held and thus the one who holds it. The institutions and systems that prop us up with sticks that we consider markers of respect are happy for us to haggle over shadow shape and size because that has no bearing on the fire continuing to rage. In fact, the flames spread wider and lash more fiercely until our own legs are alight, but in a haze of toxic fumes we remain diverted towards asking that our features be better imitated by the shadows.

In this quest for 'more accurate' representation, we have accepted the premise that it matters more that our shadows are discernible than that we are safe from being burnt alive. This means we have conceded to being reduced to puppets.

I think of a BBC Radio 4 podcast that interviewed me in 2018. It was called *How to Be a Muslim Woman*. I hated the title and wanted to critique it by arguing that the show should focus less on us and more on the state violence that impacts 'how' we are able 'to be' 'Muslim women'. Subsequently, I prepared myself with great fear of being misconstrued. I went to the interview equipped with a double-sided sheet of notes. I was chuckled at, but it was important to me not to say anything that could be co-opted, and I felt I had achieved this. However, when the whole podcast came out, although it was true that my interview was left largely unedited, the very next episode featured a Muslim woman whose story was all about joining the military. So what had I salvaged?

Presumably, the aim of including both of us in the podcast series was to demonstrate the multiplicity of 'ways' one can 'be a Muslim woman'. A critic of state violence *or* part of its machinery. But what does this do? Show that we, too, can persecute on the state's behalf? Although the series may have shown that our shadows come in different shapes and sizes, the fire that sets the world ablaze through military violence was left to burn on because it was this that allowed us to cast shadows at all.

Being invited to add kindling to such a fire is not something to celebrate. Whether it's Rishi Sunak or Suella Braverman or whoever will come next, inclusion within violent systems is not the furthest horizon we can hope for. This is at best a boring place to be, static and self-essentialising, and at worst, it is collusion with the status quo.

If we consider it more important to be able to name and assert our identities than our demands, where are we headed? And if we tie our demands directly to our identities rather than the conditions that create them, what change can we expect?

For instance, there is no word for 'Asian' in most 'Asian' languages. So whilst we clamour for better or bolder 'Asian' characters or ministers, aren't we letting our claims be dictated by a limiting Eurocentric worldview that will always denote 'Asian' as Other?

Or when we celebrate our post-colonial nations' independence days and seek to hang flags in classrooms or street corners, on some level aren't we accepting the imposition of borders and identities that imperial powers used to distinguish and divide us in the first place? Aren't these so often the very same structures that perpetuate mass violence to this day and that ought to be reminders that the colonial project is ongoing, not 'over'?

What if, instead of resenting the inaccuracy of demographic data questions, we resented the fact that we are coerced into making our claims for resources and accountability on grounds of identities that have themselves been forced on us? If we must frame our demands for better pay on account of our being 'BAME employees', for example, we are cornered into inhabiting a social position that exists solely in relation to Whiteness. This makes the knot of racism one that we become more enmeshed in, not less. When we cling to these categories, we end up reifying and reinforcing them rather than disrupting their role as the vantage points from which to seek justice and make demands.

Even the backlash against the term 'BAME' is often limited to asking what less offensive term we should use in its place. We rarely consider that instead of naming ourselves in relation to white supremacy, we could name white supremacy itself. Rather than 'BAME employees', what if we talked about 'White institutions' and 'White employers'? What if we identified the unnamed operation of power that imposes identities on us instead of consenting to these names that aren't our own? What if we refused to be puppets? What if we refused to care about the shapes of our shadows? Maybe then we could focus on extinguishing the fire. Or better yet, collapsing the cave!

I don't want positive representation, I want my childhood back. I want the parents in prison to come home, to have come home already, to have never left. I don't want positive representation, I want the planes to open back up their bellies and re-internalise the bombs. I want Faheem Qureshi to get his eye back. I don't want positive representation, I want my time back. I want to have never memorised a justification for why I wear it. I want to have never felt smallness. I want to walk with giant steps. I want my sorrow to be a headline. I want our deaths to be devastating. I want the world to stop. I don't want positive representation, I want tyrants on their knees, I want yawm al-qiyamah. I want more than IPSO apologies. I want the Channel to dry up. I want our siblings to stride through the seas and claim what's theirs. I want them to take it all back. I want homes unburied by rubble. I want the shrapnel reconstituted into a body of metal never to touch a baby's skin. I want torsos with no memory of being pushed against car bonnets. I want the journalists jobless. I want economic losses.

I don't want positive representation.

Faheem Qureshi was a fourteen-year-old victim of the first drone strike ordered by President Barack Obama on 23 January 2009. He lost multiple members of his family and suffered serious injuries, including the loss of an eye.

Call me unsupportive or hypocritical, but I hate watching TV shows with Muslim protagonists. The pressure of communicating a 'Muslim identity' is writ large through them in a way that makes me sweat. The authenticity drive stifles their capacity.

Perhaps if a thousand TV shows with Muslim protagonists existed, each one might not feel so painful. As it stands, the prevailing representation of 'Muslims' on British TV is that of Muslim men of South Asian heritage (whatever that means), and unfortunately, I have rarely enjoyed what I've seen. The standard narrative of these shows involves parents, elders or a community with 'restrictive cultural norms' and a protagonist who wants to escape them through rebellion against religion or the pursuit of white women.

You might suggest that my lack of enjoyment is because I am uptight and have the wrong sense of humour, but I would suggest that it is because I have a sense of self. It angers me to repeatedly see Muslim men assume that by centring themselves they are transgressing white supremacy's Islamophobic gaze, when their own gazes erase, exclude and belittle the women in their lives. Sisters, mothers, aunties, daughters and grandmothers become silent collateral. I do not mention wives or partners in this list simply because I cannot think of a single storyline involving an Asian Muslim man who has chosen an Asian Muslim woman as his love interest.

In fact, the presence of Muslim women in these shows often serves only two purposes: to soften the representation of the Muslim man—showing he is paternal, protective and redeemable, not merely the embodiment of your projections—or to reinforce Whiteness as the object of love and the gaze being sought.

Beneath the surface of my hatred of such shows, though, is pain. Because if I am honest, I feel betrayed. To me, these stories simply represent brown men's fantasies of having the same agency that white men have, because for once, the man usually labelled only terrorist, only honour-killer, only corner-shop owner, paedophile, inmate, suicide bomber or torturer finally gets to access masculinity on whiter terms: in the ability to objectify a white woman on screen for all the world to see.

This is not liberation. This is a puppet-man pushing a puppet-woman towards the cave wall just to make his shadow look bigger next to hers.

But in my hurt I am doing the very thing that shadow-play wants us to do. I am overlooking who is pulling the strings of those puppets. Who chooses which stories are commissioned, which shadows will be cast? What are the financial dynamics behind their decisions? How much agency do the writers that I berate have in the writing rooms of large production companies? Who directs the final shots? Who tweaks the script?

It is ironic that my pain could prevent me from accounting for the puppet masters when I first came to write this. My oversight speaks to the fact that we struggle to make room for complexity even when we think that we are doing so. I have always tried (and more often than not failed) to push myself to hold multiple truths, because doing so makes for more rigorous solutions. In my view, simple answers reveal either insincerity or an inability to contemplate one's own complicity in the world, whereas if two or more things can be true at once, we have to think harder.

So I cannot simply distance myself from the men I feel pained by, but rather I must see them as being amidst a fire just as I am. I cannot solely condemn them as perpetrators while viewing myself as a victim, for they too are victims in their own way. I must be able to feel the betrayal that I feel but also understand the context of the deeper wound—our shared wound. I will not pretend that holding both things is easy, but it is necessary to work towards collapsing the cave.

In fact, creating space for complexity would see the edifice of 'representation' come crumbling down, because we would then have the breadth of understanding to say that it is moving when a Muslim child is overwhelmed by seeing someone who looks like them on TV, but that this does not change that child's likelihood of falling into poverty at ten times the rate of the wider population.[3] We would be able to say that it sometimes feels rebellious to see people of colour in positions of power, but that the only real rebellion consists of rupturing processes of power themselves.

In fact, the purpose of representation needs to be disconnected from world-change altogether. Representation cannot be our route to justice or even superficial 'equality', but that does not mean it has no value. I think the point is best made in the work of my friend Oluwatosin Daniju, a photographer and artist who made a portrait series of Black women called *You See Yourself?*[4] At the exhibition opening, she explained that the series had initially come about from the intention to 'represent', but she soon realised that it mattered less for others to see the pictures than for the women to see themselves. Not to see themselves because others do not, but to see themselves for themselves.

Similarly, in her book *Black Looks,* about Black women in film, bell hooks wrote, 'How they see themselves is most important, not how they will be stared at by others'.[5] This made me wonder, what would it look like for a TV show or play to exist in which a Muslim woman simply saw herself? Where her relationship to herself and her Creator mattered more than how anybody else saw her?

Or indeed, a show that was not about presenting Muslims as *also* desirable and reformable, but in which we desired *one another* and desired good for one another. How the world saw us would not matter; all that would matter would be how we saw each other: as beautiful, a means of getting closer to Allah. Wouldn't that be transgressive? Wouldn't that do something else to the gaze other than simply replace it?

But perhaps I am wrong again. The mere fact of airing such a show on mainstream television would likely compromise its potential. After all, how can our looking at one another be solely for ourselves if it is watched by an audience? Do we need to be seen seeing ourselves?

The complicated truth might be that it does feel good to see a shadow of yourself at times because it reminds you that you are solid enough to cast one. And, if we're honest, the warmth of the fire is alluring because the world can be a cold place. But it is also true that there is no hope of putting the fire out if we never address it. And there is no hope of living if we remain in the cave.

Indeed, whether it is Plato or al-Ghazali who is right about whether the exterior of the cave is attainable in this life, the fact of Surat al-Kahf remains: a cave is not a place to stay forever.

ACT I: SCENE III/
INTERLUDE

AFTER *FAIRVIEW* BY
JACKIE SIBBLIES DRURY

a group of five Muslims enter the stage—mixed ages, ethnicities, genders. They approach a table with scripts on it. It should be unclear whether this is a scene or an interlude, or whether it is even part of the play, because none of the other characters are present.

A fire burns in the middle of the room. **the group of five Muslims** *pick up the scripts. They are blank.*

(The five characters are labelled 1–5.)

1   There's nothing here

2   I don't get it

3   There's no story?

1   Well—nobody's written one

4   So what are we supposed to do?

5   Who are we supposed to be?

1   I'm not sure

2   I've never thought about who I'm supposed to be if there's no script

4   Maybe it's not who we're supposed to be but who we *can* be

5   Who can we be?

3   We can be anyone

2   Anyone?

3   Well, we can be ourselves

Pause.

2   Who is 'ourselves'?

3   I—I'm not sure

1   Well, who were you before all the scripts you read?

5   Do you remember?

4   Maybe we don't need to remember—maybe we can
       just start now

1   Start being?

2   But they're watching—they're expecting

3   They're always expecting

2   But what I mean is I don't know how to be *myself* if
       they're looking

1   I know what /you mean/

4   /Because/ I'm still wondering what they think
       and that matters because it has real-life consequences

5   I know

4   I know

1   What if we asked them to close their eyes?

2   I don't think that would be—
       I still want to be seen
       but seen as in understood
       not just looked at

5   Yeah, not just /looked at/

3   /Not just/ /observed/

4   /Not just/ a thing to be watched

1   Yeah, a person

2   A person who looks, too

4   What if we—can we raise the lights, so we can see the audience?

1   What happens if we look back at them?

2   Let's look

House lights turn on; the fire turns off (it was artificial). The cast should ad-lib a bit here, wave at anyone they recognise, etc.

5   Bit weird, isn't it?

3   Yeah, there's still /something/

4   /Well, it's that/ we're up here and /they're/

1   /Yeah,/ /it's still/

2   /Imbalanced/

4   It's always been imbalanced

Pause.

2   What can you see?

3   I can see what you can see

2   No, but name it

4   Name what we can see?

2   Yeah

4   Well, I can see you guys

2   What else?

4   I can see
      white people looking at us

2   Anything else?

5   I see white people's faces
      I see them not smiling

I   They're wondering whether to accept this
      accept us looking

Pause.

3   But didn't we just accept it when they looked at us?

Curtain suddenly falls. There is the sound of something smashing or a ceiling caving in.

End scene.

BEYOND PUPPETRY

Many of us who have grown up racialised in Western contexts go on a similar journey. In broad brush strokes, it looks something like moving from the desire to be acceptable or unproblematic to Whiteness, to becoming repulsed by our internalisation of that gaze, to deriding Whiteness for its violence. Then we attempt to reconstitute ourselves without Whiteness as our aspiration, searching for new forms of belonging, home and meaning. This often leads to co-opting or romanticising contexts abroad without acknowledging global realities and the nuances of our own complicities. And in this, we inadvertently accept the premise that we do not belong, are homeless and unmeaning without Whiteness, despite thinking we rejected it.

On noticing this contradiction, we begin to say, *No! We have as much meaning without Whiteness! We, too, are artists, joyful, beautiful, intelligent! We were kings and queens once!* We reconstruct our value outside and independent of Whiteness, not in relation to it anymore, we think. But this focus on parallelisms keeps us in its shadow, and its history, trying to write a catch-up story.

I am bored of this. Bored of always being in relation to or attempting to escape relation to Whiteness. When giving talks and facilitating workshops in recent years, I have therefore urged people to think about 'who we are on our own terms'. But I am beginning to realise it is more difficult than expected to escape relativity entirely. It baffles the mind to think of oneself on completely independent terms. After all, we tend to understand things according to what they are not: I am alive because I am not dead. It is day because it is not night.

Subsequently, my pursuit became less about attempting to define myself without relation to anything and more about being in relation to something beyond Whiteness. Could there be another barometer? Something bigger? For me, this question brought me to what has always been before me, the biggest thing of all. If I consider myself to be a soul prior to being a body, then the thing I am primarily in relation to is not Whiteness, which objectifies my exterior and makes me an 'it', but Allah, who knows my interior.

I started to explore whether existing in relation to Allah alone could be the escape from existing in relation to Whiteness. Allah as the Creator, myself as created. Allah as the All-Powerful, myself as powerless. Allah as the Provider, myself and all of creation as provided for.

Astoundingly, in considering what possibilities opened if I saw myself in relation to Allah above all else, I recognised these *were* my own terms. At this recognition, I felt myself both exit and enter a cave, moving from a Platonic cave of deceit to a cave of devotion. From a cave where I was bound to the diversion of shadow and light and what I could see with my eyes to a cave where I might seek closeness to my Creator with my heart. This was a relation that clarified the range of possibilities I face. Rather than striving to be seen, approved or understood by gazes that shrink me, all I have to do is that which brings me closer to my Maker, who sees the full context of me. Everything else is either a means to this or a diversion from it.

In fact, there is a hadith reporting that the Prophet ﷺ said to his close companion Abu Bakr (may Allah be pleased with him), 'Oh Abu Bakr, there is idolatry among you more hidden than the crawling of an ant.' Asked how to avoid such unnoticeable idolatry, the Prophet ﷺ advised making the following supplication:

اللَّهُمَّ إِنِّي أَعُوذُ بِكَ أَنْ أُشْرِكَ بِكَ وأَنَا أَعْلَمُ وَأَسْتَغْفِرُكَ لِمَا لَا أَعْلَمُ

Oh Allah, I seek refuge in you from associating partners with you whilst I know, and I seek your forgiveness for when I do not know.[6]

The word 'idolatry' brings many things to mind, but in Islam it relates to deifying or worshipping anything other than Allah—any violation of Allah's Oneness. Obvious examples include worshipping an idol made by your own hands or deifying a human being. But idolatry can also include more subtle deification, such as worshipping one's own desires. Therefore, the above narration is invaluable in reminding us that we could be invested in idolatry that we are completely unaware of.

It seems obvious that Whiteness fits the description of an idol on that basis. The white gaze has so normalised its place on the pedestal of our minds—as our value-marker and meaning-maker—that it has essentially been deified. Living in relation to or not in relation to Whiteness is therefore a waste of life at best, and at worst it consists of reverence and worship of something other than the One who made us.

LATER

Yesterday I suggested to myself that the greatest idol is the white gaze, as evidenced by our lining up for MBEs and OBEs; patting ourselves on the back for wearing hijabs in places of power; gripping hands with royals. But today, I am thinking about what Tarek Younis wrote, that 'the greatest idol will always be the self's yearning to be seen'.[7] Now I find myself thinking *that* might be closer to the truth of it. After all, did Whiteness make itself an idol, or did we make it one in our desire to be seen by it?

Pleasing Allah alone requires letting go of the desire to please others that assert a god-like claim to power over us. But there are few worldly desires so strong as the desire to please, and thus be seen by, power. This underpins so many other desires—for wealth, status or awards. And importantly, Whiteness is not the only gaze of power that the self yearns to be seen by. For example, those who seek Islamic knowledge rarely aspire to a white gaze, which does not see such knowledge as legitimate, but there are still seductive and incentivising gazes at play. For although it is hoped that the goal of knowledge-seeking is to please Allah, Allah Himself cautions throughout the Quran against chasing the lure of financial reward, public approval or institutional recognition, which nullifies such pursuits.

This is interesting to consider as it suggests that although we may not be driven by the same gazes, our aspiration to be seen could have the same root. I think back to a 2019 boycott that I was involved in and the fallout around it. I was among a number of people who withdrew from participating in a literary festival because we considered the festival's acceptance of government counter-extremism funding to amount to the

79

dangerous normalisation of the policing of Muslims in the arts. Media coverage framed our withdrawal as undermining, even intimidating, a grassroots festival, but in 2022 the festival founder received an MBE, showing that being 'seen' by power in this way led to material benefits and that our disruption had only had a minor impact.

But I want to hold the mirror up to myself for a moment to make a different point. I might smugly dismiss those whose actions I consider to be seeking the gaze of Whiteness and institutional prestige, but what gazes do I seek that betray an insincerity in my own heart?

Can I say with full conviction that my ego was not stoked by the approval of our boycott in the gazes that I place on my own pedestal? Can I honestly say that being deemed to have integrity and principles by people that *I* value did nothing to my initial intention? Can I say that there was not a part of me that felt recognised in its own way by being castigated as the 'radical' and 'dissenter'? Would recognition of myself in this way even be possible if I weren't seen in relation to others, whom I perceive as the 'non-radicals' and 'reformers'? And is investing in that relation not just stooping to define myself in relation to something other than Allah?

What righteousness can there be in toppling Whiteness from its pedestal only to customise my own idols? Different gazes, but the altar is the same: the self's yearning to be seen.

BEYOND THE CAVE

I want to take us somewhere beyond these circles of self-deception. I no longer hope to be see-er or seen; I want to run in another direction altogether. Neither to the past for proof, nor to the future for possibility, nor side to side in parallelisms and alternative gazes. I want to move another way: beyond. After all, that is the direction of the soul's aspiration, no?

It seems that as a Muslim, I cannot exist on this plane except in relation to Whiteness, the war on terror, other Muslims labelled as 'radical' or 'moderate' or some other reference point. But when this world is rolled up like a scroll, I will exist as a Muslim on the only plane that ever mattered. And this is where it becomes easy to answer the question of who I am on my own terms and how I might be that. The most effective way of breaking away from the dichotomy of existing either for others' eyes or for myself in relation to them is to exist for Allah's gaze alone.

But what would it look like to exist for Allah's gaze alone? To escape and surpass the gazes of others?

I used to struggle with this, but perhaps it is not as difficult as I once thought. The truth is probably that the only way to exist for Allah's gaze alone is to practise it. That's it. I can write myself into circles of admission and realisation and it can still all be posturing. I can perform it for the praises of others. I can say it to make it appear that this book exists with good intention. But the only way to live in the sight of Allah is to do it. A reality that cannot be seen by others.

How perfect.

The very act of sincerely existing for Allah's gaze alone is one that might not and could not be recognised by others.

Therefore, it undermines the performance of existence because it does not require it.

It is to be in the cave of devotion without anybody knowing you are there.

To be in the cave of devotion in your heart even whilst you are in the cave of deceit in body.

To exist for Allah alone is the strangest possibility.

حروف مقطعة

The huroof muqatta'ah are disconnected Arabic letters that appear in the Quran at the beginning of some chapters. The scholars do not agree on their meaning.

Let us be like حروف مقطعة
disjointed letters
unwilling to bend to be words
sounds of a kind, though unheard

Let us be unintelligible!
Unrepresented
the الٓمٓ (alif, laam, meem)
let no expert know what we mean

Let the scholars disagree if we are pronouns
or simply syntax
reference, reason, or just stand-in
then let the puzzle be abandoned

Let us be strange
and okay with it
leave us awardless and uncelebrated
leave us wherever the hereafter is

Let us be secret meanings
known only to Allah
no consensus, no agreement
leave that as our achievement

δ

ESCAPING THE CYCLE /
EVEN STRANGER
POSSIBILITIES

ACT II: SCENE I

Back in the library, which is almost completely water now. **the book** *is cradling* **the writer** *as tears gush from* **her eyes** *(closed). She is using* **her heart** *to see, and* **her fear** *has been allowed back through the doors—she sits on* **the writer's** *chest.*

the book	Can I do anything to help?
the writer *sobbing*	Yeah, don't— don't be for anyone
the book	Don't *be* for anyone?
the writer	Yeah let me put Muslims inside you who are Muslim but don't let anyone see them keep them hidden let there be no sight of their prayer mats no dhikr beads let them make sujood in another room

her fear exhales and nods with pleasure.

the writer	And make them laughers
the book	Laughers?
the writer	I want them to laugh to laugh and smile because it's the sunnah
her heart	And because the sunnah is the sunnah!
the writer	Exactly! And that's enough of a reason It never has to be stated, but *we* know

her heart looks closely at **the writer** *and* **the book**. **her fear** *is shrinking by the second.*

the book   I think I can do that

the writer   Oh—and let them look at each other
          but somewhere we can't see

the book   Okay

Pause.

the writer   Thank you, by the way
          for holding me when I'm like this and
          well, for not leaving me on my own

الغيب

AL-GHAIB (THE UNSEEN)

In Islam, belief in الغيب is fundamental to faith. That includes believing in Allah, the angels, the holy books, the prophets, unseen entities, the hereafter and predestination. Faith is conditional upon this.

'Belief' and 'faith' are loaded words, though. They connote a lack of certainty. Some sort of opting in. But that is not the way this feels. And as a child, it is as easy as breathing. There is no doubt that Allah, angels and any number of unseen things exist. What child does not believe in the unseen?

But as I entered the social world of secularism's norms and derision of God-centred epistemologies, I realised there was meant to be shame attached to this belief. Certainty in God's existence was not cool or clever. And it definitely wasn't deemed a satisfactory justification for your choice of dress or your decisions to participate or not to participate in activities at school or anywhere else outside your home. In fact, it made you the antithesis of what an 'intelligent' student was supposed to be. It made you stand out awkwardly: weird PE kit, weird uniform, weird diet. Constantly placed in a position where you had to disprove that you were a bizarre sight. Constantly in a position where you had to shrink your belief in God.

As a child I knew how this made me feel, but I could not understand it then as I can now. الغيب, the unseen, falls outside of the secular-colonial-liberal paradigm in which the 'real' is only that which is observable and measurable. Ironically, this is despite that same paradigm's reliance on its own unseen: terrorist bogeymen, phantom job-stealers, the spectre of marauding asylum seekers, and weapons of mass destruction that never appear. But while belief in racial essentialism escapes intellectual disparagement, belief in الغيب is painted with marks of backwardness.

If we overlook this inconsistency for a moment, we can see that the mainstream narrative about modern Western philosophy is that it doubts the existence of what is not observable. René Descartes famously theorised 'cogito ergo sum'—I think, therefore I am—the notion that the quintessential certainty is of one's own existence, because that is the prerequisite for thinking, and therefore for doubt itself. The senses, perceptions and all else might be unreliable, but the fact that a person has doubt means they must exist. This first principle, a thinking mind, then serves as a basis for finding out if other truths are certain.

However, those who accept Allah work from a different premise. Rather than the idea that our thinking is the foundation upon which all other knowledge and belief is built, we have the notion of the divine command, كُنْ فَيَكُون, kun fa-yakoon, 'be, and it is'. Things exist because Allah orders them to 'be'.

This is another paradigm. To take Allah as the premise of everything else, rather than as a hypothesis to be tested by our own 'cogito', is to live a different reality. It is a reality I have rarely discussed before, but the extent to which my day-to-day life is guided by that which I cannot see is immense.

From my belief in a day that is coming, my hopes, my dreams, my conversations with those who aren't here anymore, my secrets buried and my shame, fear and hurt, to my belief in angels, jinns, 'ayn and hasad, and in Allah's presence, love, trust and knowledge of my intentions, my interactions and routines are informed by a whole world that surpasses my thinking. It can alter how I walk down a street, the greeting I give someone, why I might go back to pick up a piece of litter, and my choice to hold or not hold my tongue, delete a tweet, wash my hands or stand my ground. In fact, upon consideration, the seen world is barely as motivating or explanatory as the unseen world.

I go to sleep reciting Ayat al-Kursi (the Verse of the Throne) to ensure an angel stands guard over me throughout the night. I wake at dawn compelled by a reward based only on a promise from the Unseen. I turn my head right and left after worship to greet the two noble scribes who write down my actions and deeds throughout the day. I wipe my hands over my body after blowing prayers into them to protect myself from devils and envy. I whisper words as I enter the bathroom to seek refuge from evil forces. And I write this wondering which actions to declare or not to declare so as to protect my intentions, unseen.

Moreover, Muslims are motivated not only *by* the unseen, but also to *be* unseen, because the best actions are those carried out purely for the sake of God. Hence, charity is considered likely to be more sincere, and more accepted, when given privately and prayer when offered in the middle of the night, because these deeds' intentions are least defiled by the gazes of others. Simultaneously, we are cautioned against swerving too far the other way by stopping worship or good deeds for fear of doing them to impress others, as this can lead to disobeying Allah for the sake of people. Instead, the median is encouraged—intend well with all that you do. The reason for this is found in a hadith reported by Abu Hurairah (may Allah be pleased with him), who said that the Messenger of Allah ﷺ said, 'Verily, Allah does not look at your appearance or wealth, but rather He looks at your hearts and actions.'[1]

This narration encourages us to preoccupy ourselves with inner refinement, rather than merely to *appear* spiritually superior. After all, how many robed men have acted in ways that disappoint? How many Muslims inflect our speech with 'insha Allahs' and 'masha Allahs' only to be hollow underneath the skin? How many times have we chosen to impress total strangers with our selflessness while mistreating the people closest to us? And how often are tyrants lauded whilst the friends of God are persecuted and blamed?

These questions guide me to the strangest possibility so far. Beyond the desire to be seen by people is the possibility of being content with being estranged from their gazes; of going *unseen* by others because you recognise that is how to be seen in the best light by the Unseen One who sees you best.

This is not to say we abandon one another—no. It is rather that we recognise there will be limits to our ability to see each other truly.

We should still strive to see one another; serving and caring for others and being in community are means of pleasing Allah. Excessive ascetism is discouraged in Islam, as is shunning the people. But to be content with going unseen could open a more subtle possibility. I can still seek to see and love others and can still yearn to be seen and loved by others, but if I embrace the idea that what I keep between me and Allah alone may be the most valuable of my deeds, a window is created wherein going unseen is not a tragedy but an advantage.

This feels like the best way to exit the diversion of 'representation', for example, because behind closed doors, in my room, on my prayer mat, I am not a 'Muslim woman' waiting to be reflected back to myself—I am just a soul relating to Allah. When we're secluded from the distractions of the world and other people, the realisation that we are never truly *alone* is clearest. And in this, there is no demand to be seen. In fact, when unseen by human beings—'alone'—I feel most seen by my Creator. Most free.

This also releases us from the need to be surveyors of ourselves as objects. Instead, we aspire to observe ourselves in order to remember that we live in the sight of Allah, and thus to remind ourselves to act ethically, to improve, to rectify our behaviours and to take account of ourselves. This reveals that self-scrutiny is not inherently harmful. It is only violent when we are monitoring ourselves on behalf of a corrective white gaze, a punishing secular gaze or a sexually objectifying gaze, because in those cases we are disciplining ourselves to please *them*.

Instead, Allah's gaze aims to make us excellent. We see this in the famous hadith in which the Angel Jibril (or Gabriel) appeared to the Prophet ﷺ and his companions as a man and asked, 'Tell me about ihsan (excellence)'.

The Prophet ﷺ replied,

أَنْ تَعْبُدَ اللَّهَ كَأَنَّكَ تَرَاهُ، فَإِنْ لَمْ تَكُنْ تَرَاهُ فَإِنَّهُ يَرَاك

Excellence is to worship Allah as if you see Him, for if you do not see Him, He surely sees you.[2]

Living solely for the sight of Allah aims to improve us. It brings the limits of our own sight into question too, because *we* are not the determiners of our excellence. And how could we be? Even when light enters the pupil of the human eye, it forms an upside-down image on the retina which is translated into a right-side-up image by the brain. Our sight does not capture things 'as they are'. Or, as one of my teachers often quotes, the fault is in our eyes, not in the stars.

In other words, seeing with our own eyes, even if they could be stripped of the gazes we internalise, would not enable us to perceive things as they really are. Indeed, our eyes were never ours to start with; they are gifts and means of interpreting reality, but the only true sight is with Allah.

Therefore, instead of endeavouring to 'be seen' *or* to 'see for ourselves', a surer way to surpass the problem of gazes is by deferring sight completely to Allah. When I think of this, the following hadith qudsi (a narration by the Prophet ﷺ in his own words but with meaning revealed by Allah) comes to mind:

My servant draws nearer to Me with nothing more beloved to Me than that which I have made obligatory upon him. And then My servant continues to draw near to Me with optional acts (nawafil) until I love him. And when I love him I become the hearing with which he hears, and the sight with which he sees, and the hand with which he smites, and the foot with which he walks. And if he seeks My protection I will surely grant him My protection. And if he seeks My victory I will surely grant him the victory.[3]

In this hadith, Allah tells us we have the ability to draw closer to Him and be loved by Him through acts of worship, and that His love of us will manifest in His becoming our hearing and our sight. This final point interests me most for this discussion. As much as we can only come to wildly deficient conclusions about what it might mean to see with Allah's sight, it is clear we would benefit from it. Allah's sight is obviously superior, whilst we can only see that which Allah has chosen for us to see. Can we see honesty? No. Sincerity? No. But Allah sees our hearts, intentions and insides. And if He so wills, Allah can bestow light upon our hearts to see things as they really are.

It becomes clear to me now that what I was seeking in my attempts to archive, record and witness myself, in performing, refusing to perform, and everything in between, was only ever truly attainable through the sight of the Maker of all things. It is only in Allah's sight that I can be truly, deeply seen, and it is only by deferring to Allah's sight that I may truly begin to see.

In fact, the declaration of faith that a person makes to become Muslim (I bear witness that there is no god but God, and I bear witness that Muhammad ﷺ is the Messenger of God) is called the shahadah, الشهادة, from the root letters ش ه د, giving meanings of witnessing, observing or seeing. It is less a declaration of 'belief' than a confirmation of what one has seen beyond the limits of one's eyesight.

اللَّهُمَّ أَرِنِي الْحَقَّ حَقًّا وَوَفِّقْنِي لِاتِّبَاعِهِ وَأَرِنِي الْبَاطِلَ بَاطِلًا وَوَفِّقْنِي لِاجْتِنَابِه

O Allah, show me the truth as truth and guide me to follow it.
Show me the false as false and guide me to avoid it.

AL-BASEER (THE ALL-SEEING)

البَصِير

al-Baseer (noun): the One who sees everything; one of the ninety-nine attributes of Allah.

بَصُرَ / يَبْصُرُ / بَصَرَ

basura, yabsuru, basar (verb—Form I): to look, see; to realise, understand, comprehend, grasp.

أَبْصَرَ / يُبْصِرُ / إِبْصَار

absara, yubsiru, ibsar (verb—Form IV): to see, catch sight of, behold, discern, perceive; to notice, observe; to make out, recognise; to try to discern or perceive.

تَبَصَّرَ / يَتَبَصَّرُ / تَبَصُّر

tabassara, yatabassaru, tabassur (verb—Form V): to envisage, regard; to try to get an insight; to consider, ponder, reflect; to gain or have a keen insight.

إِسْتَبْصَرَ / يَسْتَبْصِرُ / إِسْتِبْصَار

istabsara, yastabsiru, istibsar (verb—Form X): to have the faculty of visual perception, be able to see; to be endowed with reason, be rational, reasonable, intelligent; to reflect, ponder.

And yet I falter again.

Although I have found a way of fulfilling my desire to be truly seen by relating only to Allah, and although I have found a way to surpass the goal of seeing with my own eyes by deferring sight to Allah, there is still a limitation to my understanding. The number of times I have typed 'I' and 'my' speaks to the fact that I am still centring *myself* in all of this.

I critiqued Descartes for his 'cogito'-centred approach to the world, but is mine any less ego-centric? What would it mean to abandon my obsession with myself and instead recognise that everything that happens to me, all that I see and experience, is a manifestation of Allah's power, mercy, might and planning?

What if I could see only Allah? What if, beyond *my* desires, *my* hopes, *my* wants and *my* choices, I was able to see Allah's will and design? Allah alone. Allah the Reality. Allah the Truth.

This possibility is even stranger.

It helps me to understand my relationship with others better, too. In rejecting their gazes because they violate my ability to exist primarily in relation to Allah, I am not rejecting others entirely. No. In fact, love is one of the most determining factors in my life, and I have chosen to share stories of love in this book in order that they be witnessed.

So it seems to me that there is a type of triangulation at play. Maybe in loving and attempting to see and be with one another, there is a possibility for a communion that can bring us closer to Allah, too. After all, part of trying to see Allah alone is to see Allah as the One behind everything that happens and everything that is. In that case, part of truly seeing one another is to see God as each other's mover, originator, protector and creator.

Perhaps with our hearts in the cave of devotion and our bodies in the cave of deceit, we could observe the people around us as insights into and means to Allah. I think of congregational prayers and remembrance. I think of communal fasting. And I think of the prisoners in Guantanamo Bay.

In a written testimony of his experience in US custody at Guantanamo Bay, Jumah al-Dossari recounts a time when a man was praying the duha (mid-morning) prayer and therefore did not reply to a warden who told him to take off a towel he had wrapped around himself for modesty. When the warden subsequently interrupted the man's prayer and pushed him to the ground, Jumah relays that the other detainees began to shout 'Allahu Akbar' (God is greater) in unison. He writes, 'all the camps started to say "Allahu Akbar"; the whole place echoed with chants of "Allahu Akbar".'[4]

I get goosebumps when I think of this moment and others like it. Men coercively excluded from the sight of others through detention in far-flung corners of the world recognising that they are each other's earthly witnesses, and that Allah is their only real witness. Seeing one another as a means of seeing *only* Allah. Seeing one another's forced invisibility and pain as a means of remembering that Allah, unseen, is greater than any whim, wish or power of our own. That Allah is greater than all, vaster than all, encompassing all. That the reality before them was one of deception, but the reality they called upon was True.

Jumah testifies that when the Muslims began to chant 'God is greater', 'the soldiers started running away. One soldier was driving an armoured cruiser outside the camp, [and] when he heard "Allahu Akbar", he turned the cruiser and got down from it and started running.'

Allahu Akbar.

الصديق

AL-SIDDIQ (THE TRUTHFUL)

Al-Siddiq was the title given to the Prophet Muhammad's ﷺ closest companion, Abu Bakr (may Allah be pleased with him), after an incident in which members of the Makkan community came to mockingly tell him of the miraculous night journey the Prophet ﷺ had made.

Aishah (may Allah be pleased with her) reported:

> They sought Abu Bakr and they said, 'Have you heard that your friend imagined he was taken by night to the sacred house [in Jerusalem]?' Abu Bakr said, 'Did he say that?' They said yes. Abu Bakr said, 'If he said it, he has spoken the truth.' They said, 'Do you believe he went by night to the sacred house [in Jerusalem] and returned [to Makkah] before morning?' Abu Bakr said, 'Yes. Verily, I believe what is even more astonishing than that. I believe he has received messages from heaven for everything he does.'[5]

Abu Bakr said this to a community who did not dispute the notion of God, but he was still deemed absurd for his commitment to faith. Yet, instead of trying to rationalise the claim of the Messenger ﷺ, apologise for it or reduce it to a symbol, he held his head high and said, *if he said it, then it is the truth, I believe him without explanation, and I also believe that which is even more improbable, that which is even stranger.*

To me, such a stand is an act of limitless bravery. It is to say that you do not need the affirming gazes of others or to be legible, comprehensible or known to them. Instead, you are willing to be mocked and ridiculed, not only unseen but the worst type of sight: an absurdity. All because the only sight you live for is that of Allah, and because you are committed to His Messenger ﷺ.

Abu Bakr knew—and knew that it seemed extraordinary—that his friend the Prophet ﷺ received revelation from Allah. He accepted this truth because he had known the Prophet's character ﷺ for years and, as did all who knew him, knew that he was only ever truthful. Indeed, before his prophethood, the people of Makkah had nicknamed Muhammad ﷺ 'al-Amin', meaning 'the trustworthy'. Therefore, when the Prophet ﷺ told Abu Bakr that he had started to receive revelation from Allah, Abu Bakr believed him completely.

By the time of the incident of the night journey, Abu Bakr's logic was clear: if the Messenger of Allah ﷺ said he had travelled 800 miles in one night, it was true. Legible or illegible, comprehensible or not. Abu Bakr's measure of truth was not based on what was thinkable to *him* (may Allah be pleased with him); it was based on what came from Allah and His Messenger ﷺ and on his love for the Messenger ﷺ. This was his epistemology.

Indeed, this is not solely a story of commitment to truth. It is a story of love as a commitment to another's truth, even when we cannot see it with our own eyes.

Do we dare to be that committed to truth? To abandon the quest to be seen, in preference of the unseen and unexplainable? To prioritise love as a form of witnessing that is higher than sight? To prioritise love of God and His Messenger ﷺ as our way of knowing?

In the second Hijri year (624 CE), between 313 and 317 of the first Muslims gathered in the valley of Badr in the Arabian Peninsula against a force of around a thousand from the Quraysh clans who sought to destroy them and their subversive religion. The Muslims were incredibly ill-equipped for fighting, and thus the non-Muslim forces assumed they would win an easy victory. But in the end the Makkan forces were overpowered by the smaller force, and the reason for this victory, as agreed by both sides, was the presence of angels.

An army of 3,000 angels was sent by Allah to fight with the Muslims at Badr.[6] In many reports of the battle, both Muslim and non-Muslim eye-witnesses recount seeing unknown horsemen whose horses' hooves did not touch the ground; or hearing voices urging them forward; or seeing the enemy flee from ones other than them.

It probably reflects badly on me to admit that in my childhood my imagining of this battle was made most vivid after I watched *The Lord of the Rings: The Return of the King*, in which Aragorn arrives to save the day with an army of glowing green ghosts—an army of the dead. Of course, angels are not dead men, but the presence of invisible, invincible forces that smite the enemy on behalf of our protagonists made the stories seem similar when I was a child.

I know this comparison will reinforce the disbelief of some readers. I understand some will baulk at the idea of angels assisting in a battle—indeed, at the idea of angels at all. But I also know that I believe in even stranger stories than this one and that you, dear reader, do too.

For instance, I know someone who was never very good with deadlines, neither was he particularly religious at the time. So on the eve of a major deadline, when he stayed up well into the night, it fell to his mother to pray for him. She prayed to Allah to send angels to bolster the boy in his final hours of writing.

Just as an army of angels was sent to the battlefield of Badr, she asked that they be sent, now, to a bedroom in the north of England.

By the morning, not having told her son of this prayer, she checked in on him and found him reviewing what he'd written, impressed with himself. He said he almost felt as if he hadn't written it. At some level, in fact, he did not remember writing through the night at all. He was sure that, gripped by exhaustion, he had just slumped at his desk. But reading over the work, he was amazed at the writing. The argument was more cogent and lucid than he had imagined. It didn't even sound like him, he said. And so, the mother told him the truth of her supplication.

Whether angels did or did not write the student's undergraduate dissertation does not concern me. What astounds me is that a boy who had been so sceptical of faith up until then was genuinely of the opinion that a host of invisible forces could have written his dissertation. And that a mother held her child's dissertation to be a cause deserving of angels.

The angels are not the most unbelievable part of this story. It is the bewildering, invisible force of love and care that a mother had for her child, and the inconceivable change of heart that a young man experienced overnight. For which is more improbable? That angels aided a boy to write, or that one day he would have mocked the very idea of angels and the next could concede that they were possible authors of his work?

Whichever answer you land on, I guarantee that you probably believe in something even stranger.

In the istikharah prayer for guidance, we implore Allah to guide us and make the best option clear and easy for us. We say, *You know and I do not know, and You are the knower of the unseen.*

بَدَأَ الإِسْلاَمُ غَرِيبًا وَسَيَعُودُ كَمَا بَدَأَ غَرِيبًا فَطُوبَى لِلْغُرَبَاءِ

Islam began as something strange, and it will return to being
strange, so blessed are the strangers.[7]

The noun 'stranger' means strange one; unfamiliar; unrecognisable; unknown; puzzling; provocation; not from home.

The root letters of the word غريب (strange) are غ ر ب, which,
as a verb (غَرَبَ), can mean to go away, depart, withdraw; or, with
a different pronunciation (غَرُبَ), to be a stranger; to be odd,
obscure, difficult to comprehend.

*

There is nothing comparable to praying with strangers.
Hearing the call to prayer distantly draw to a close, the congregational worship about to begin, you push yourself between
the shoulders of women you have never met before to fill gaps
in the rows. Their sides jostle with yours as your feet attempt
to choreograph a formation with them.

Somebody pulls your elbow closer; another adjusts your
scarf. There is an intimacy that is impossible with strangers
elsewhere. And that's the point. The strangeness is surpassed
by the knowledge that your purpose is singular. Not only here
in this moment, when you are about to raise hands to ears and
declare that God is greater. But here in this world, where you
are all deficiently striving to set sights on the One who is other
than yourselves, to remember that God is greater. Here in this
world, where you are all struggling to be columns of fortitude
despite being wobbly on your legs.

In the company of strangers, between their shoulders, you
recognise that you, too, are simply a stranger. That you are just
a shoulder to somebody else, just a leg pressed against a coat,
just a breeze of a whispered prayer. And in this is the possibility

of both things: that you do not matter beyond this moment of closing the row to make a stranger's prayer rewardable, and that you matter just as much as every furrowed brow around you, that you are just as flawed, just as short-sighted, just as intimately messy and trying, and just as loveable and worthy of compassion.

When we stand before Allah, what will it matter what Islam means beyond the meaning of the word itself?

أَسْلَمَ / يُسْلِمُ / إِسْلام

aslama, yuslimu, Islam (verb—Form IV): to submit oneself to the will of God.

مُسْلِم

Muslim (noun): one who submits oneself to the will of God.

٦

GRIEF IS A
TYPE OF GHAIB /
LOVE IS A TYPE
OF SIGHT

ACT II: SCENE II

The stage is drowned in grief. Nothing is above its waters. Global geography has taken an afternoon nap so the whole thing is dislocated.

her soul *is light the whole way through this scene, though not visible to the audience; this shouldn't even be conveyed.* ***her eyes*** *are pacing back and forth as* ***her heart*** *lies spread-eagle on the floor.* ***her head*** *doesn't need to be in this scene but inevitably is hovering.*

her eyes	Why are you doing that?
her heart	Sorry I just need just need a rest
her eyes	From what? I'm the one who's always guarding you
her heart	Good one! You're the one that takes everything in!

Pause.

her eyes	Oh gosh, sorry Here, let me

her eyes *close.*

her heart	You know I'm not blaming you, right? It's not your fault that I get heavy sometimes
her eyes	I know Sorry, I don't know why I'm getting all watery about it
her heart	It's okay to do that, you know

	In fact, sometimes I need you to
her eyes	You do?
her heart	Yeah, so that things can grow and so *I* get a chance to see, too

Pause.

her eyes	You can do that?
her heart	Better than you'd believe

Eye contact with a stranger, sometimes an eye roll, even the most fleeting of nods has often been what made it possible for me to escape objecthood when nothing else could. I have stood on the brink of it. Being folded into the smallest thing imaginable. Crashing towards the inevitable loss of agency, autonomy, self—and then someone catches me. A stranger holds my gaze and in that, they stop the fall. I suddenly have two feet on the ground. I suddenly have a gaze that can be held. And if that is true, I am not just a sight.

No matter how small it feels to witness someone sometimes, it is still something. Something that says, *I see you.* I see *you* beyond the sight. I see you not just with my eyes but with my heart. I am looking with my heart.

And is that not the clearest sight? As Allah says,

فَإِنَّهَا لَا تَعْمَى ٱلْأَبْصَـٰرُ وَلَـٰكِن تَعْمَى ٱلْقُلُوبُ ٱلَّتِى فِى ٱلصُّدُورِ

So indeed, the eyes are not blind, rather the hearts which are in the chests are blind.[1]

On board a plane to America in 2018, I watched an uncle accidentally hold up an entire queue of passengers in his struggle to sort his bags out. Murmurs started to build, and I felt myself begin to crumple on his behalf. There was no way for me to speed him up, nor to intervene in the looming frustration targeted at him. But near the end of his plight, he looked up from the bags, eyes searching, and settled his glance on me. In that moment I understood that all that was needed was my witnessing. All that was needed was the assurance of my sight. Not the sight of my eyes—for there were so many on him—but the sight of my heart. A type of looking that said, *I understand.*

I smiled, and he smiled back.

*

It is reported on the authority of Abu Sa'id al-Khudri that the
Prophet Muhammad ﷺ said,

مَنْ رَأَى مِنْكُمْ مُنْكَرًا فَلْيُغَيِّرْهُ بِيَدِهِ، فَإِنْ لَمْ يَسْتَطِعْ فَبِلِسَانِهِ،
فَإِنْ لَمْ يَسْتَطِعْ فَبِقَلْبِهِ، وَذَلِكَ أَضْعَفُ الْإِيمَانِ

Whosoever of you sees an evil then let him change it
with his hand, and if he is not able to do so then with
his tongue, and if he is not able to do so then with his
heart—and that is the weakest of faith.[2]

There is an oft-quoted section of an ayah of the Quran where spouses are referred to as 'garments' for each other:

هُنَّ لِبَاسٌ لَّكُمْ وَأَنتُمْ لِبَاسٌ لَّهُنَّ

They are a garment for you, and you are a garment for them.[3]

The metaphor of a garment is a profoundly generative way to understand love. Something that covers you, holds you and protects your nakedness, from the root letters ل ب س, which link to concepts of clothing, enveloping, surrounding and accompanying.

Perhaps the type of sight that doesn't require escape to your bedroom is the sight that can make a person, or people, a sanctuary for you in and of themselves. Sight that holds you in your incompleteness. That witnesses you at your most vulnerable and covers you.

I began this book concerned that anything that I ever write relating to myself is not my story alone—that none of our stories are. For this reason, my choices to cover or reveal, to protect or uncover, are choices about love and how to hold the ones I love who are a part of me, whose yarns weave in and out of mine.

Muslims are told to begin all acts with the words 'bismillah al-Rahman al-Raheem':

بِسْمِ ٱللَّهِ ٱلرَّحْمَٰنِ ٱلرَّحِيمِ

In the name of Allah, the Most Compassionate,
the Most Merciful.

Is it not more merciful to look with the heart than with the eyes? Is that not a type of covering? Is that not a type of holding? Are we not all incomplete and vulnerable and yearning to be held by a gaze that doesn't constrain but protects? And can we not try to be that for each other?

After all, we are told we should attempt to emulate the qualities of Allah, and one of Allah's ninety-nine names is العفو, al-'Afw, from the root letters ع ف و, which point to meanings encompassing forgiveness, pardoning and removal. In the Arabic language, the word is sometimes used to reference the way wind wipes away footprints with its blowing. Metaphors are gifts from God that can help us to bridge the unfathomable. So, although we cannot comprehend Allah truly, al-'Afw suggests one who wipes away not only a person's errors and faults, but even the traces of them.

If there is a merciful erasing of erasure, then this is it. Not the institutional burial of evidence to avoid accountability, but the covering up of human, intimate slips to instil hope and remind us of our own fallibility.

Islam urges us to have clemency—to do better to others than they have done to us. Of course, this becomes complicated on the scale of global power dynamics and could easily slip into a troubling case for political quietism. But concealing each other's flaws is not the same as acceptance of state-level injustice. When it comes to those we love, if Allah—who sees all—veils and hides our shortcomings, then who are we—who see so much less—to withhold this same grace from one another, especially when we ourselves are in desperate need of cover?

A poem of Imam al-Haddad comes to mind, in which he addresses Allah, saying:

يَا عَالِمَ السِّرّ مِنَّا
لَا تَهْتِكِ السِّتْرَ عَنَّا

O knower of our secrets,
do not remove [Your] protective veil from us.

If we are seeking to truly live for Allah, then isn't love of one another and acceptance of each other's incompleteness incumbent upon us? Is it not a means of understanding that Allah's covering and Allah's love are greater than anything we can imagine?

Recognising ourselves as imperfect is how we know Allah as perfect. Recognising ourselves as interdependent is how we recognise Allah as independent. And acknowledging our imperfection and dependency is surely the very thing that enables us to recognise that Allah *is* greater.

'ALHAMDULILAH FOR THIS SPACE WE'VE BUILT TOGETHER'

—DR AZEEZAT JOHNSON[4]

There was a time when we never spoke on the phone. Two years perhaps. But we exchanged twenty-minute voice notes in which we told each other how seen we felt by the other. I can't listen to them anymore, not yet.

At that time, I had not seen you physically for almost three years. I had briefly watched you on a Skype call here and there, but when I basked in your voice notes in my walks around the park, I felt seen and saw you best, most clearly.

In each other's voices we built closeness. There's something about the meandering of voice notes that allowed us to witness the most vulnerable parts of each other's thinking—the mistakes, the rewinds, the uncertainties. It was an intimacy of its own. Somewhere we learnt to see each other not with our eyes, but with our hearts.

Which, in some ways, made your leaving easier. And in some ways, it made it harder.

The story of the Prophet Yusuf (or Joseph) (peace be upon him) is widely known. When Yusuf was a child, his brothers threw him into a well out of jealousy of their father's love for him. Upon returning home, they fabricated a story that their brother had been killed by a wolf. In the Quran it is then told how their father, Yaqoob (or Jacob) (peace be upon him), responded:

وَتَوَلَّىٰ عَنْهُمْ وَقَالَ يَٰٓأَسَفَىٰ عَلَىٰ يُوسُفَ وَٱبْيَضَّتْ عَيْنَاهُ مِنَ ٱلْحُزْنِ فَهُوَ كَظِيمٌ

And he turned away from them and said, 'Alas my grief over Yusuf!' And his eyes became white from the sorrow that he was suppressing.[5]

*

I am neither a scholar nor a commentator, but this verse always makes me think about the morning my grandmother awoke with partial sight. The doctors told her that she had such severe scarring on her eyeball that it seemed as if she had witnessed an explosion. My grandmother has never witnessed an explosion, neither that night nor any other night. Or perhaps it is truer to say that we have never witnessed my grandmother witness an explosion. Not one that happened externally anyway.

*

قَالُوا۟ تَٱللَّهِ تَفْتَؤُا۟ تَذْكُرُ يُوسُفَ حَتَّىٰ تَكُونَ حَرَضًا أَوْ تَكُونَ مِنَ ٱلْهَٰلِكِينَ

They [the brothers of Yusuf] said, 'By Allah you will not cease to remember Yusuf until you become fatally ill or become of those who perish.'[6]

قَالَ إِنَّمَا أَشْكُواْ بَثِّى وَحُزْنِىَ إِلَى ٱللَّهِ وَأَعْلَمُ مِنَ ٱللَّهِ مَا لَا تَعْلَمُونَ

*He [Yaqoob] said, 'I only complain of my suffering and my
grief to Allah, and I know from Allah that which
you do not know.'*[7]

*

I think of all the unseen complaints of suffering and grief that
God alone hears. It is the invisibility that can make grief most
difficult. The fact there is no fanfare upon the loss of someone
we love. The traffic does not stop. The world keeps spinning.
The grief is buried in the body.

In fact, scientists have found that experiences of loss can
cause migraines, chest pains, heaviness in the limbs, aches in
the neck, back and skeletal joints. The entire body can become
inflamed. An inferno of white blood cells is sent to protect the
body from attack where there isn't one. At least, not one that
is visible to the naked eye. And yet, despite its invisibility, it is
something so powerful it can turn the sight receptors white.

White the colour of absence? Or white the colour of pain? I
associate white with hospitals. Clinical white, alarming white,
bright white. One Ramadan we prayed in the mosque close
to the hospital where Nana was having to spend the month.
The imam made a prayer that all those in hospitals be healed. I
thought about how invisible the inside of a hospital feels until
your life becomes entwined with it. A world unto itself. Much
like a prison. Much like a detention centre. Much like a heart.
Much like a grave.

I accidentally read two books about grief on a sunny June afternoon. Afterwards I am scared to open WhatsApp because I will see you there, still reassuring me you will reply properly in a few days. As I re-write this paragraph, I notice the date. Exactly six months since you left.

I remember following your body—in the hearse—to the burial ground. I was so aware of your presence ahead of us. The air felt laden with your soul. I could almost see you and the angels attending to the matters at hand.

A man with a bunch of flowers paced the rows of headstones behind us as we stood watching you—your body—become unseen. I heard him make a phone call. *I can't find Mum.* I wanted to tell him, no one can help you with that now.

Lorraine Hansberry wrote, 'The acceptance of our present conditions is the only form of extremism which discredits us before our children.'[8]

I read this quote in the opening of bell hooks' book *Black Looks* only recently. It caught my eye because it is so forceful. I immediately googled Lorraine Hansberry and must admit, with shame, that that afternoon was the first time I heard of her. Born in the 1930s, she was the first African-American woman to have a play produced on Broadway. It was called *A Raisin in the Sun*, the title inspired by a line in Langston Hughes' poem 'Harlem': 'What happens to a dream deferred? / Does it dry up / like a raisin in the sun?'[9]

Captivated, I found and read *A Raisin in the Sun* over the course of a few bus journeys. The story became interspersed with excerpts of conversations I heard on the bus: the hopes of old men, ailing women and children, all waiting for someone to pull through or for something extraordinary to end the wait on their dreams. I thought about the continued deferral of dreams, and about my friend who taught me the most about dreaming, and about the fact she is no longer here.

James Baldwin said that Hansberry's play was the first in the 'entire history of American theater' to have 'so much of the truth of black people's lives'.[10] After Hansberry died of pancreatic cancer in 1965, aged only thirty-four, he wrote, 'it is not at all farfetched to suspect that what she saw contributed to the strain which killed her, for the effort to which Lorraine was dedicated is more than enough to kill a man'.[11]

My friend who taught me about dreaming also died from cancer, just months before I read *A Raisin in the Sun* and days before her own thirty-fourth birthday. My friend was also a Black woman, and I know that what she saw contributed to the strain which killed her. In fact, she told us so. Being therefore moved by Hansberry's story, I found myself wanting to tweet the quote from her, that 'the acceptance of our present conditions is the only form of extremism which discredits us before our children'. But I faltered.

I faltered because I know that I cannot say with certainty that the 'present conditions' of which Hansberry spoke are conditions that I have played no part in producing—or, at the very least, in accepting as default. It was my friend Dr Azeezat Johnson who talked about anti-Black racism as a default carelessness. What does it mean for something to be default? It is when you buy a new phone and the screensaver is already set. It is the automatic premise. The assumed beginning. To change it you have to make a decision; you have to change the entire set-up.

When I assume that my desire to reject our present conditions is the same as Hansberry's desire, what do I refuse to see? Whom do I overlook? What parts of her do I force to be silenced?

Don't get me wrong. I am not arguing against broad-based solidarities; I am aware of the usefulness of 'strategic essentialisms' when used alongside commitment to anti-essentialism more broadly. But I am also aware that when Nina Simone wrote the song 'To Be Young, Gifted and Black' in Hansberry's memory, she was not writing for me, nor was she writing for Gayatri Spivak.[12] I understand that this doesn't mean we cannot listen, but as someone who has written poems for specific audiences, I know that it also means that Simone did not care for my consumption of the song. It is excess. And if it can be that—excess, secondary—then I am not, in fact, in the same boat as Hansberry, or as Simone.

And so, I faltered to tweet the quote not because our conditions are not shared, nor because I accept them, but because they are not shared in the same way. My friend was thirty-three and dying, and I was twenty-seven and dying, but we were not dying in the same way. And now her soul has taken flight from this world. Do you see?

FOR AZEEZAT JOHNSON

You wrote about the tent as a metaphor for building a collective together. And then you wrote about us letting go of the tent and laying down on the earth and being held by her.[13] You wrote about how we might be able to both tend to the earth and let her tend to us. Now you are in her, and I wonder if that is not poetic.

And yet it is not *you* you, but the worldly you, the body of you. The *you* of you is in another version of this plane, another plane altogether. But I still reach you via prayer, I hope. I still mention you before dawn. I still sit in our conversations, knowing you are urging me to think further, to feel deeper, to take my thoughts and unspin them, to sit in my body and listen.

There was never going to be enough time, no matter what. There never could have been enough time with you. You, who made us wiser and slower. You, who called me to be braver than ever before. Who held hands with me even when we knew it was hard. Who showed me that love is not about what you do *for* each other, but what you do with the difficult parts of what you have been taught to do *to* each other.

You are still in my walks around the park. I would record and listen to our voice notes there, and part of me still would now. There is so much to tell you about. Every day there is more. Ironically, I find myself wanting to talk to you about grief because I know you would have so much to say.

Sometimes it is enough to know what you would probably tell me in response to such thoughts. Sometimes that stops me short and gives me the answer I didn't know I was looking for. But other times, the not knowing is what sits on me. Not knowing is the hardest and best thing I learnt to do with you. It is so much harder to do without you.

I am trying to live up to who you believed I could be even when I wasn't. If that is not the impact of grief/love, I don't know what is. Sometimes now when I speak to a crowded room, I am actually only speaking to you, feeling you witness me and knowing you would tell me there is space for all of it: the general and the specific, the love and the hurt, the hope and the despair.

People think it is hard to give up on love—to drift, to let the ways we wound each other become a chasm that separates us. But I think it is harder not to give up on love. And your generosity and faith in love and in letting it hold us to account made loving you one of the most important things I have learnt to do so far in my life.

People often quote that line by blogger Jamie Anderson, that 'grief is just love with no place to go'. And I get it, but I disagree. The love has so many places to go—in fact, the love must go every place. Which, in turn, means you do. Every act of love I undertake is informed by love of you. That love doesn't sit and turn to grief; instead it imbues all the rest of the love with the colour of you. So now all my love and all my attempts to love are inseparable from what you taught me of love, and how we loved one another, and all of it is all of it. And all of it is you.

Another of my friends is dying now. In fact, if I enumerated how many have skirted death's edges already, I would not want to share. But this friend, she is dying in a different way.

I went to deliver a birthday card to her on her ninety-first birthday but learnt she was in hospital. When she came home I visited her. She wanted to show me the exercises she has had to do for her legs since the fall. She led me up to her pink bedroom using a walking stick and leaning heavily on the banister. She lay down slowly and stared up at the ceiling. I couldn't help but think about how like a skeleton her face looked at that angle. Skin almost transparent. How the transition to lifelessness seemed mere moments away.

There is something both endearing and ugly about nearness to death. I understand why we cringe away from it. Who wants to believe that one day the highlight of their day will be lying on a mattress raising their legs in the air? Who wants to think that one day they might be lying face down on their own landing at 4 a.m. shouting for a neighbour to help them? Nobody wants to disappear before they have.

I have known this friend since she was eighty. She is a white woman. She told me back then, when we met, that the hardest part of aging was having lost her husband thirty years ago. His absence was in every corner of the house. Winter evenings were the worst, she said, because when you closed the curtains you felt doubly alone.

One day she brought a book downstairs for me. An English-to-Urdu dictionary. His. He'd been placed in India in the 1940s. She told me he said that Kashmir was beautiful. I said I wouldn't know and tried not to think or speak on it further. My friend explained that when he returned to Leeds, in the 1960s, her husband had used his Urdu to help translate for families at the school I would attend forty-five years later. I sat, conflicted.

When my friend came home from hospital after her birthday, she left me a voicemail. In it she simply said, please come and see me, I'm having a terrible time. *See me. I am having a terrible time.*

I wonder if being seen is the antidote to a terrible time. Maybe in some small way. But we both know it is no guard against death. So these days when I visit my friend in the care home that she has had to move to, I wonder at the simplicity of our interaction. I go to see her. That is all. I cannot stop the tide of what is coming and nor can she, and neither of us knows when the last visit might be. But there is something in that practice of going to see her that still does something. Something that stops her from becoming invisible. Something that stops her from becoming a stranger to this world before she has left it.

There is a tender intimacy that I have been privy to with the women in my family: massaging, oiling hair and other embodied rituals that have never existed with men. So, when one day I took charge of trimming my grandfather's beard, it brought me closer to him than I had ever been before. It is likely that I hadn't touched his face in almost twenty-seven years, or at least not since being a baby. Placing my hand on his cheeks and gently shearing the white hairs of his beard, I was surprised by how soft his face was. It had never occurred to me that he would be soft to touch. Almost like a child. As I cupped his chin in my hand and tilted his face to reach every part of his beard, it also occurred to me that in fact he was, once, a child.

Nana has become more legible to me with age. Where before he would not speak a word, he now cries for minutes at a time. No shame in that. But as he has become opaquer, his world has become vaguer to us. At one point he began to sleep upside down on the bed to face the door, a dozen suit jackets tucked under the duvet beside him, to keep them safe from robbers. The robbers came by night. Nobody else saw them but we still helped him fortify the house. That is what you do when you believe in the reality of another's unseen. You do not have to believe it is real—whatever real is—to know that it is real for somebody else. You still listen attentively because it is the telling of the story that matters most, or how you receive it.

Sometimes Nana tells us not to change the subject. We are simply following the online advice to gently distract, but sometimes distraction feels as underhand as saying *we do not see you*. For several weeks in August, Nana kept telling us that a pigeon had fallen from the roof of the house next door. It fell at night and was struggling to get up. I would often say something like *how strange*, or *really?* But one day I looked over and said *I can't see anything.* With certainty, he replied *abhi aap ko nazar ayega—you'll see it any second now*. And I realised that he was right. Any second now a day might come when I see fallen pigeons where others do not.

After a while, we grew to see that nothing about Nana had really changed. What can be seen with the naked eye is barely anything at all. Because the eye cannot see the things which move us most. Especially love.

There is a storyline from one of my family's favourite TV shows, *Lost*, where the character Desmond becomes unmoored from time and his consciousness begins to 'time-slip'. One moment he is in the same timeline as the other characters, trapped on an island, and then in an instant he flashes into his own past yet with the consciousness of his 'present' self. He opens his eyes in a helicopter over the Pacific Ocean in 2004, then blinks and is in the middle of a military-training drill in Scotland in the 1990s.

The week the crocuses emerge in Leeds, something very similar begins to happen to Nana. One instant he is sipping tea in his armchair and the next he is urgently informing us that the traffic light is about to change and he needs to release the handbrake. Telling him he is at home in the living room is no comfort.

Upon witnessing this, my mother finds new meaning in a memory she had not previously understood. When she was a child, an old woman would occasionally knock at their home asking for her laundry back. My mother would tell the woman that she had not left any laundry and that in fact this was not a launderette at all. But the woman was adamant. She would plead to the point that my mother would grow scared and close the door.

Remembering this woman now, my mother becomes sad. She wishes she had not been afraid. And yet it is difficult to resist fear when somebody does not consent to our reality as the only one. It threatens our sense of certainty. It exposes the fragility of our experiences, revealing the unseen to be merely a moment away. Merely the distance it takes to forget something. Merely the time it takes to remember something.

To sit with someone who is physically in the same space as you but consciously elsewhere makes the reality of the grave much easier to comprehend. It shows us that there is little reason to think the person in the grave is not alive in ways other than in body. In fact, it makes more sense to understand them as merely a slip away. It makes more sense to consider that if a moment could fracture and fissure and split to reveal all of its dimensions, we would see the person in the grave and their reality right before us.

And won't a moment fracture and fissure and split to reveal all of its dimensions for all of us some day?

In Urdu, they say someone or something has become ghaib if they disappear from the room or go missing.

Grieving someone whilst they are still present is a strange way to relate to the ghaib. I met a man who reminded me of what my grandfather might have been like fifty years ago. I felt a strange ache in my chest. A yearning for some time or place that is no more. I wanted to tell him, *my granddad lived here, too. These streets knew him better than they might even know you.* I wanted him to hear Nana's name and light up in recognition. I wanted Nana's absence to be noticeable.

There was a time when Nana could not walk down a Bradford street without being stopped and spoken to. I have a half-memory of watching the scene unfold from beside his legs, my small hand held in his. I felt that this must be what fame was like. And he was made for it. He seemed to be able to hold everybody's greeting for just the right amount of time, ask questions about the right family members, reminisce about the right incidents. An encyclopaedia of community, recipient of home-cooked meals, hand shaken by all.

When I turned seventeen, Nana gave me my first driving lessons. An instructor for many years by then, he knew the streets of Bradford better than he did any parcel of land on this earth. People would wave when they noticed his car come by. Years later, he would leave the house one day and be recognised by a passing driver, who would pull up and say that he had been taught by him. Noticing Nana's slow gait and a certain amount of confusion, the driver would ask if he needed a lift home. Thankfully, everybody knew where my granddad lived.

But now, with this man who somehow reminded me of how Nana might have been fifty years ago, when I tried to explain that these streets know me, that they know me through Nana, that they love him, love us, the man simply said that the motoring school's name rang a bell, but he couldn't put a face to it.

TO HOLD THEIR MEMORIES

AFTER JOSE HERNANDEZ DIAZ

I fell off my bike and hit my head enough to cause a mild concussion. When I woke the next day, I found myself able to access the memories of everyone I had ever loved. I was able to understand them so fully that it broke my heart. I became hesitant to open myself to new people because in knowing them I would come to love them, and in loving them I would come to hold their memories. I began to see my mother's childhood like a storybook open before me. Painful traumas she could not recollect fell into my open palms. I saw my grandparents before migration. The wedding day they could not recall. Childhoods they would cover up with time. I listened to the humming voices of workers on a factory floor in Bradford. I felt the uneven ground of paths I could not distinguish from my own. I was able to lose myself just falling into the memories of those I loved. I gracefully attempted not to see their shame. I let memories of guilt and humiliation wash right by me. This was a gift, but it was also a burden. My fatal flaw is that I think I understand people just because I can contextualise them. But the truth is that people are not lists or Excel spreadsheets, and so my capacity to love them exceeds my capacity—and indeed does not need my capacity—to know them.

I did not anticipate that this book would include a section on grief, but it makes sense, because what is the desire to be seen if not a desire to not be dead? And what is the desire to evade death if not a misunderstanding of reality itself? And what is reality itself if not the unseen? And what is the unseen if not the very essence of our lives? And what is the essence of our lives if not love, care, hope, pain? And what are love, care, hope and pain if not our attempts to see one another? And what are our attempts to see one another if not the very nature of being human? And what is the very nature of being human if not struggle? And what is such struggle if not the thing that makes life worth living? And what is the thing that makes life worth living if not the hope to see Allah with your heart, and if not that, then at least to know that Allah sees you? And what is such knowledge if not a resolution of the desire to be seen? And what is resolution of the desire to be seen if not willingness to go unseen? And what is the willingness to go unseen if not a freedom from this world? And what is freedom from this world if not leaving it?

V

A NOTE ON ENDINGS /
THE IMPOSSIBILITY
OF CONCLUDING

ACT II: SCENE III

We are no longer under water; the library has completely disappeared. **the writer** *sits writing the book at a booth in a café, drinking chai.* **her eyes**, **her head** *and even* **her soul** *share the booth with a sense of calm.* **a group of five Muslims** *laugh in a booth beside them, though the audience cannot see them.* **her eyes** *stay closed but* **her heart**—*some way apart from the rest but encompassing the entire scene—is wide open like daybreak.*

There is a sense that this moment exists outside of time, which is no longer a metaphor for anything.

her head	I think I understand now
her eyes	What?
her soul	No, not like that She means **the book**
the writer	You're a journey, aren't you? Not a depository
the book	Yeah you make me, but you don't determine me you had to let me look at you so I could see beyond you

Pause.

the writer	I don't know how to end you
her soul	Well, you can't know how to do something you haven't done yet yourself
the writer	Ending?

her soul *nods wisely.*

the book   Just end me honestly

*her fear spills out of **the writer**'s chest upon the utterance of those words. They all stare.*

her heart   Okay, yeah
                     I suppose that's a start

*her heart laughs and laughs until **the writer**, **the book** and **her eyes** are recognised as irrelevant. **her soul** takes leave of **her head** and **her fear**, and **her heart** takes the path.*

ME

AFTER JOELLE TAYLOR

When they search me they are showing me myself
This is your writing, unsatisfactory
colour of humiliation
something you sought to capture escaped from the jar

Here is your self
your soul and your heart
both too vulnerable and too arrogant, let's pack them away
these eyes though, they were never yours

They begin to open a flat-pack white box
press along the folds
say, this is for you
a place to stay

And suddenly I recognise that they are me
they go to lift me into the box
but now I am floating
more like exploding
more like exceeding

I hear a voice that must be my own
for are all of them not mine?
It shouts

Call me absurd! Call me utopic!
Call me rigid and myopic!

Call me orthodox, call me toxic!
Call me egregious and boxed in!

Call me too flexible and fallible!
Call me a show-off, call me intangible!
Call me obvious, call me cringeworthy!
Call me overbearing with victim mentality!

Just do not call me only one thing
I could not bear to be only one thing
for that is worse
far, far worse
than being absolutely nothing at all

When I lead creative writing workshops, I enjoy inviting participants to imagine that the world has been changed in all the ways they believe it should be, and then I ask them what it looks like.

Children do well at this. They tell me about treehouses and endless play, exclaim about limitless stretches of green and invincibility. Young people also do all right. They speak to me about a world of free movement, healing for all, fully funded well-being services, freedom to pray where they want and conflict resolution that does not rely on punishment.

Adults hesitate. I pre-empt their fear of imagining by telling them not to worry about how such change would happen but instead to focus on what they would see. They hesitate again. They begin to reproduce only the least worst of what they have already seen. Imagine only absences, not presence. No more litter, no more cars, no more pollution. They imagine a blankness, empty space. No more shouting, no more poverty, no more inequality.

They cannot tell me what they do see. Perhaps they cannot see how to see. And this is not a problem per se, for we cannot be blamed for an inability to imagine what we cannot imagine, but our dreams cannot only be absences. Our aspirations cannot only be lack-of.

I ask them: if I showed you an acorn and told you it would one day become a towering body of wood filling the air and sky and stretching branches over crowds; a home to birds, to squirrels, to life; an anchor for an ecosystem; a source of food and fuel and shade and firelight ... would you believe me?

Then what of us? What might we yet become that we cannot even conceive as possibilities? What might we yet dream of that we cannot even begin to speak? How might we yet see, with closed eyes? And how would such seeing with our hearts open possibilities beyond even our strangest imaginings?

WHEN THE TREES BEAR
WITNESS ABOUT ME

Everything is a witness and will give witness; that is what we understand. Our arms, our legs, our skin, tongues, hands and feet. Testifying against us—or, ideally, for us.

But today I am thinking about the trees. I am thinking about how much a tree has seen. How often I have thought I am walking down the tree-lined boulevard of the park and gazing upon them, when they have been gazing upon me.

I am astounded by all they have seen of me. Every age of this body, every range of emotion. I think of the friendships that have carved curling spirals through and around those trees. I think of the exam results come and been celebrated in their midst. I think of the denim cuffed and scuffed with tree bark from the climb up, then perched atop with a book—my idea of the height of summer, the height of freedom. I think of every version of me-on-wheels they have seen. The summer of skateboards, the roller blades, the first time I cycled without stabilisers, the thousand times I have cycled since.

I think of the tears they have seen. I am embarrassed by the conversations they have heard. With friends, with colleagues, with people with whom I was trying to establish what we might be. The phone calls, the voice notes, the meandering monologues to a friend now gone, but whom they, too, were witness to, and so who is not lost entirely.

I think of the outfits! The styles! The fashion! Think of the luminous green skinny jeans! The patchwork knitted jacket from TK Maxx that I adored until somebody at school asked if my grandma had made it for me. The ill-fitting dresses, the Eid attires. How many picnics? From the average sandwich to the day we brought aloo parathas with tava in tow to keep them warm. Think of the ice creams! The Flakes! The inflation of the cost of a 99!

What do they think of me, these trees? How would they judge me? When they speak, what will they bear witness to of my well-trodden paths and intentions? What do they know of me that nobody else does? What would they say of me that nobody else could?

In almost every audience Q&A at events I am invited to speak at, somebody asks me about hope. Where do we derive it? How do we get it? What happens if we can't find it, or worse, when we lose it?

I marvel that they assume I have such an abundance of it. But I think that is exactly the point. I often say that hope is incumbent upon us, because to despair would be to doubt Allah's ability and power, and besides, despair only benefits the status quo.

I do believe that, but the more basic answer is to be found in the asking of the question itself: we get it from each other. Just sensing that somebody else has hope encourages us to source it, too. Ironically, this means hope is both contagious and bottomless, an infinite well.

Even contemporary researchers into 'hope', such as psychologist Shane J. Lopez, have found that it is 'dependent on your entire social network' and 'shared with others'.[1] Lopez describes hope as 'the golden mean between euphoria and fear ... the feeling where transcendence meets reason and caution meets passion'.[2]

When I encountered this concept of a 'golden mean' between euphoria and fear, I was reminded of a saying attributed to Ibn al-Qayyum:

> The heart on its path to Allah the Almighty is like a bird, where love is its head, and fear and hope are its wings. If both the head and wings are sound, the bird will be able to fly properly. However, if the head is cut off, the bird dies; and when the bird loses its wings, then it is susceptible to every hunter or predator.

Being suspended between hope and fear may then be the only way to maintain hope. A seeming contradiction, but one which makes sense upon reflection. Hope on its own could only exist in a world of total safety and justice. And in such a setting, what would be the need for hope in the first place? Would we not speak only of contentment there? Of رضا? And is that not the very essence of Paradise?

In our world, hope on its own is surely foolishness. We speak of fearless hope sometimes, but I do not believe those whom we deem fearless are ever truly fearless. Most often, the times when people have called me brave—and I have believed it— have been when I am on the brink of tears.

I think hope is like perseverance, maybe even just another word for it. I make this connection because of the saying that a believer should always be in one of two states: شكر or صبر, shukr or sabr, gratitude or perseverance. Gratitude is said to be the more difficult to maintain because you must choose it, whereas with perseverance, you rarely have another option. I would say this is also the nature of hope. It is hardest to find when fear is distant, and most palpable when fear is close.

So maybe when people ask me where we can derive hope, I should tell them that it is not in avoiding fear but in sitting with it, holding its hand, bending so close to touch it that hope is the only possibility left.

Indeed, that is where I have found myself at the ending of this book. I have struggled to write a concluding chapter because I keep attempting to supress the wing of my fear, fear that I cannot bring all my thoughts together or sum myself up definitively. Those may be valid fears, but they come from an impossible place. I cannot end this book in the traditional sense because this book has charted a journey that I am still on. And since I am still on it, I cannot tell you how it ends.

This is a book of questions in an industry which has taught us to read for answers. But if I sought to offer 'conclusions' by excavating myself, I would be erasing the fact that I am still travelling. It would be pretending that I was writing from outside the cave when I am not even writing from outside *myself*. All I have are questions, and in questions I feel safest because the truth is that I do not know. I do not know how this book ends because I do not know how my journey ends.

But as my mother would say when cooking a handi, you keep bhunning until it 'turns the corner', which is neither a location nor an amount of time, but a recognition that the process of mixing has made the food ready. Not complete, not finished, but ready. And I hope that is where this book is, because I am not. I am incomplete and lacking. I am enmeshed in the knots of my own intentions. I am as embarrassed as I am confident. I am a bird constantly at risk of veering one way or another, merely pretending to know something of flight. And the only reason I have been able to maintain a semblance of flying at all is Allah.

As we are told in Surat al-Mulk,

أَوَلَمْ يَرَوْا إِلَى ٱلطَّيْرِ فَوْقَهُمْ صَـٰٓفَّـٰتٍ وَيَقْبِضْنَ ۚ
مَا يُمْسِكُهُنَّ إِلَّا ٱلرَّحْمَـٰنُ ۚ إِنَّهُ بِكُلِّ شَىْءٍ بَصِيرٌ

Have they not seen the birds above them, spreading and folding their wings? None holds them up except the Most Merciful. Indeed, He is All-Seeing of everything.[3]

My ability to stay suspended in the air despite careening left and right on wings of hope and fear does not come from some source of resilience within myself or the strength of my love. I am held up by none other than Allah.

This is the most honest way to end this book. Not with myself and a pretence of answers, but with Allah, who *is* the answer.

The shadows of my fears that cling to the pages of this book cannot be dissipated by me, nor by your reading it. Instead, I hold on to the fact that Allah calls Himself the Lord of the Daybreak: رب الفلق, Rabb al-Falaq. Root letters ف ل ق, meaning to split, tear asunder, or dispel the shadows of the night.

Let me end this book the way all things must end, then, with the knowledge that our sight, search to be seen, gazes, eyes, fears, hearts, souls and everything in between belong to Allah, and will return to Allah—the only thing that endures without end. The only reality. Allah alone.

إِنَّا لِلَّهِ وَإِنَّا إِلَيْهِ رَاجِعُونَ

Surely, we belong to Allah, and verily to Him we return.

اللَّهُمَّ اجْعَلْ خَيْرَ زَمَانِيْ آخِرَهُ، وَخَيْرَ عَمَلِيْ خَوَاتِمَهُ، وَخَيْرَ أَيَّامِيْ يَوْمَ أَلْقَاكَ

O Allah! Make the best of my life be the end of it, and the best of my deeds the last one; and the best of my days the Day when I meet You!

ACKNOWLEDGEMENTS

In a narration from Abu Hurairah (may Allah be pleased with him), it is reported that the Prophet Muhammad ﷺ said, 'Whoever does not thank people has not thanked Allah.'[1] I will therefore try my best to thank the people who have knowingly and unknowingly made this book possible, as all of them have been blessings Allah has bestowed upon me.

Firstly, I am clearly indebted to my nani and nana, whose lives have underpinned almost everything I have ever written and whom I have probably been shaped by more than they will ever know. Thank you, Nani and Nana, for everything, remembered or forgotten. You have taught me what true reliance on Allah looks like. Forgive me for every time I have misunderstood and for all your wisdoms that I have not recognised. May Allah grant you 'afiyah, ameen.

A major portion of this book was also influenced and informed by my love for Azeezat Johnson. May Allah grant her eternal Jannah without reckoning, ameen. Thanks also to Azeezat's family for allowing me to write about her in this book and for being so generous with her legacy.

I would also like to thank my friends Alaa Alsaraji and Oluwatosin Daniju for their art, which profoundly moves me and has brought me to important realisations about myself and my sight. Thanks to U Bava Dharani and Jess Hosie, too, whose conversations about being seen and unseen have had crucial influence on my thinking and feeling.

Thank you to Francesca Sobande, Preti Taneja, Yassir Morsi, Sabrina Mahfouz and Malachi McIntosh, not only for generously taking the time to be the first readers of my first draft, but also for sitting with it and providing such broad and insightful feedback. You enabled me to draw out the book that was sitting just under the skin of that first draft, so thank you for believing in me and seeing the hope of what I was trying to write.

I would like to take a moment to thank all my various Arabic teachers over the years who unknowingly planted the seeds of interest that sparked important connections in this book: Ustadh Mehdi, Ustadh Shamim, Ustadhah Thamina, Anse Saimah, Anse Nawar, Anse Iman, Anse Nur al-Huda, Anse Abeer, Anse Maisa, Sheikh Abu Fadil and Ustadh Salah.

I have been blessed to sit in the gatherings of Sheikh Ibrahim Osi-Efa and Sheikh Haroon Hanif throughout the journey of writing this book. Their wisdom, character and guidance have fed significantly into the book's growth, may Allah bless them, ameen. All errors and misunderstandings of their teachings are mine alone.

Thanks must go to Leeds Central Library and the Tiled Hall Café, to the chai-shop owners who did not question my bizarre presence, and to the other freeloaders who work in corporate café chains without buying any drinks. Long may we prosper!

Thanks to the Arts Council for granting me the Developing Your Creative Practice grant, which bought me the time to read and write and ponder for this book without having to take National Lottery funding or burn myself out with work.

Thank you to Hajar Press—to Brekhna and Farhaana for approaching me and trusting me to write something in the first place. You gave me a space I did not know I needed.

A special thanks to those gems who have made the risk of being seen fully feel so incredibly worthwhile. I could never have finished this book with the understanding that I have if you had not shown me that it is possible to be seen in ways beyond my imagining, even in this world. You know who you are.

Endless, eternal thanks to Sumaiyyah and Saifur Rehmaan for being the eyes through which I have learnt the most about myself. For growing with me and, despite always witnessing the worst of me, seeing the best of me.

ACKNOWLEDGEMENTS

Thanks to my mother, who is the mountain which the three of us shelter under and too often forget to acknowledge from the vantage point of her protection. No words or actions will suffice to thank you, Mummy, for how you support and love me. Your sight has been the first sanctuary I ever found, and it is the place I retreat to again and again. Please accept my constant shortcomings and forgive my ingratitude.

All praise and thanks go back ultimately to Allah, who has blessed me with an abundance of hearts, hands and teachers in my life. All error in this book is from me, and any benefit in it is from the mercy of Allah, who will have honoured me if it is accepted.

NOTES

1   It is recorded by Imam al-Nawawi, on the authority of 'Umar ibn al-Khattab (may Allah be pleased with him), who said: 'I heard the Messenger of Allah ﷺ say, "Actions are according to intentions, and everyone will get what was intended. Whoever migrates with an intention for Allah and His Messenger, the migration will be for the sake of Allah and His Messenger. And whoever migrates for worldly gain or to marry a woman, then his migration will be for the sake of whatever he migrated for."' Hadith 1, Imam al-Nawawi's Forty Hadith. Sahih Bukhari, Book 83, Hadith 66, and Sahih Muslim Book 33, Hadith 222.

۱ the need / how I am found

1   Frantz Fanon, *Black Skin, White Masks*, trans. Richard Philcox, New York, NY: Grove Press, 2008, p. xi.

2   Nayyirah Waheed, *Salt*, San Bernardino, CA: Nayyirah Waheed, 2013.

3   Hadith 1, Imam al-Nawawi's Forty Hadith. Sahih Bukhari, Book 83, Hadith 66, and Sahih Muslim Book 33, Hadith 222.

4   It is reported in Hilyat al-Awliya 13717 that Abu Nu'aym reported that Imam al-Shafi'i said, 'I never debated anyone but that I would love for him to be guided, directed, helped, and for him to be under the care of Allah and His protection. And I never debated with anyone but that I did not mind whether Allah clarified the truth on my tongue or his tongue.'

ɾ *the want / how I find myself*

1   Ian Cobain, Owen Bowcott & Richard Norton-Taylor, 'Britain destroyed records of colonial crimes', *The Guardian*, 18 April 2012, https://www.theguardian.com/uk/2012/apr/18/britain-destroyed-records-colonial-crimes, accessed 15 June 2023.

2   Shohei Sato, '"Operation Legacy": Britain's Destruction and Concealment of Colonial Records Worldwide', *The Journal of Imperial and Commonwealth History*, Vol. 45, No. 4 (2017), pp. 697–719.

3   This is exactly what happened when the existence of these records was revealed during the course of the Mau Mau lawsuit brought against the British government by survivors of torture by the colonial regime in Kenya.

4   Ian Cobain, 'Revealed: the bonfire of papers at the end of Empire', *The Guardian*, 29 November 2013, https://www.theguardian.com/uk-news/2013/nov/29/revealed-bonfire-papers-empire, accessed 15 June 2023.

5   Muneera Pilgrim, *That day she'll proclaim her chronicles*, Portishead: Burning Eye Books, 2021.

6   Quran, Surat al-Zalzalah, 99:2.

7   Quran, Surat al-Zalzalah, 99:4.

8   Quran, Surat al-Zalzalah, 99:3.

3 becoming a sight / the portal of objecthood

1   Robin Wall Kimmerer, 'Robin Wall Kimmerer on the Language of Animacy', *Orion*, 17 July 2017, https://orionmagazine.org/article/robin-wall-kimmerer-language-animacy, accessed 15 June 2023.

2   'It is a peculiar sensation, this double-consciousness, this sense of always looking at one's self through the eyes of others, of measuring

one's soul by the tape of a world that looks on in amused contempt and pity. One ever feels his two-ness ...' W.E.B. Du Bois, *The Souls of Black Folk (A Norton Critical Edition)*, Henry Louis Gates Jr & Terry Hume Oliver (eds.), New York, NY: Norton, 1999 [1903], p. 11.

3   Joelle Taylor, *C+nto & Othered Poems*, London: The Westbourne Press, 2021.

4   I have written about this at length, both on www.thebrownhijabi.com and in Lola Olufemi, Odelia Younge, Waithera Sebatindira & Suhaiymah Manzoor-Khan, A *FLY Girl's Guide to University: Being a Woman of Colour at Cambridge and Other Institutions of Power and Elitism*, Birmingham: Verve Poetry Press, 2019. In 2022, the university itself also released a report tracing its enmeshment with the slave trade: University of Cambridge website, 'Cambridge responds to legacies of enslavement inquiry', 22 September 2022, https://www.cam.ac.uk/stories/legacies-of-enslavement-inquiry, accessed 25 May 2023.

5   By March 2020, 136 charges and 92 convictions had been made under Section 58 of the Terrorism Act 2000. CAGE, '20 Years of TACT: Justice Under Threat', London: CAGE Advocacy UK Ltd, 2020, p. 43, https://www.cage.ngo/wp-content/uploads/2020/10/20-Years-of-TACT-Justice-Under-Threat-2020.pdf, accessed 15 June 2023.

6   The Counter-Terrorism and Border Security Act 2019 amended s. 58 of TACT 2000 by adding a further offence for viewing or accessing such material on the internet.

7   Rizwaan Sabir, 'Understanding Counter-Terrorism Policy and Practice in the UK since 9/11', PhD thesis, University of Bath, 2014, p. 44, https://purehost.bath.ac.uk/ws/portalfiles/portal/187958374, accessed 15 June 2023; CAGE, '20 Years of TACT', p. 17.

𝆓 striving to see / seeking subjecthood is a circle

1 Alaa Alsaraji, 'Mapping Sanctuaries', https://alsarajialaa.co.uk/mapping-sanctuaries, accessed 26 May 2023.

2 Quran, Surat al-Kahf, 18:7.

3 According to a census in 2020, 'Muslims are falling into poverty at a rate 10 times higher than the UK-wide estimation'. Muslim Census, 'Financial Impact of COVID-19 on the Muslim Community', https://muslimcensus.co.uk/financial-impact-of-covid-19-on-the-muslim-community, accessed 15 June 2023.

4 https://www.oluwatosindaniju.com, accessed 15 June 2023.

5 bell hooks, *Black Looks: Race and Representation*, Boston: South End Press, 1992, p. 130.

6 Al-Adab al-Mufrad lil-Bukhari, Hadith 716.

7 Tarek Younis, 'The duty to see, the yearning to be seen', in Asim Qureshi (ed.), *I Refuse to Condemn: Resisting Racism in Times of National Security*, Manchester: Manchester University Press, 2020, pp. 67–77.

𝄐 escaping the cycle / even stranger possibilities

1 Sahih Muslim, Book 45, Hadith 42.

2 Sahih Bukhari, Book 2, Hadith 43, and Sahih Muslim, Book 1, Hadith 1.

3 Hadith 25, Forty Hadith Qudsi. On the authority of Abu Hurairah (may Allah be pleased with him), who reported that the Messenger of Allah ﷺ said this. Sahih Bukhari, Book 81, Hadith 91.

4 Jumah al-Dossari, 'USA: Days of adverse hardship in US detention camps—Testimony of Guantánamo detainee', Amnesty International, 2005, p. 12, https://www.amnesty.eu/wp-content/uploads/2018/10/testimony_of_Jumah_al_Dossari.pdf, accessed 15 June 2023.

5   Dala'il al-Nubuwwah lil-Bayhaqi 2/361.

6   Quran, Surat al-Imran, 3:124.

7   On the authority of Abu Hurairah (may Allah be pleased with him), who reported that the Messenger of Allah ﷺ said this. Sahih Muslim, Book 1, Hadith 279.

۱ *grief is a type of ghaib / love is a type of sight*

1   Quran, Surat al-Hajj, 22:46.

2   Sahih Muslim, Book 1, Hadith 84.

3   Quran, Surat al-Baqarah, 2:187.

4   From a voice note sent to the author.

5   Quran, Surat Yusuf, 12:84.

6   Quran, Surat Yusuf, 12:85.

7   Quran, Surat Yusuf, 12:86.

8   Lorraine Hansberry, *To Be Young, Gifted and Black: Lorraine Hansberry in her Own Words,* adapted by Robert Nemiroff, New York, NY: New American Library, 1970, p. 214, quoted in bell hooks, *Black Looks: Race and Representation*, Boston: South End Press, 1992, p. 6.

9   Langston Hughes, 'Harlem', in *The Collected Works of Langston Hughes*, Columbia, MO: University of Missouri Press, 2002.

10   James Baldwin, 'Sweet Lorraine' (1969), introduction to Hansberry, *To Be Young, Gifted and Black*, p. xii.

11   *Ibid.*, p. xiv.

12   Nina Simone's song 'To Be Young, Gifted and Black' was named after Lorraine Hansberry's posthumously adapted autobiographical play. Gayatri Spivak theorised the concept of 'strategic essentialism'

to refer to a political tactic where minority groups temporarily 'essentialise' themselves to bring forward a group identity in order to achieve certain common goals. For example, different national or ethnic groups might mobilise under the banner of being 'people of colour' to articulate shared demands.

13 Azeezat Johnson, 'Starry Nights: The Evolution of Our Tent', GEM Collective website, 28 October 2021, https://gemcollective.org/starry-nights-the-evolution-of-our-tent, accessed 15 June 2023.

ᵛ a note on endings / the impossibility of concluding

1 Shane J. Lopez, *Making Hope Happen: Create the Future You Want for Yourself and Others*, New York, NY: Simon & Schuster, 2013, p. 205.

2 *Ibid.*, p. 21.

3 Quran, Surat al-Mulk, 67:19.

acknowledgements

1 Sunan Abi Dawud, Book 43, Hadith 39.